# The Terror Challenge in South Asia
# and
# Prospect of Regional Cooperation

# The Terror Challenge in South Asia and Prospect of Regional Cooperation

*Editor*

Anand Kumar

INSTITUTE FOR DEFENCE STUDIES & ANALYSES
NEW DELHI

*The Terror Challenge in South Asia and Prospect of Regional Cooperation*
**Editor: Dr Anand Kumar**

ISBN 978-81-8274-599-5

First Published in 2012



*Published by*

PENTAGON SECURITY INTERNATIONAL

*An Imprint of*

PENTAGON PRESS
206, Peacock Lane, Shahpur Jat,
New Delhi-110049
Phones: 011-64706243, 26491568
Telefax: 011-26490600
email: rajan@pentagonpress.in
website: www.pentagonpress.in

*Typeset in Garamond 11pt by The Laser Printers*

*Printed at* Agean Offset Printers, Greater Noida.

# *Contents*

## SECTION II
## Regional Cooperation in Counter-terrorism

# *List of Abbreviations*

| | |
|---|---|
| AMMAA | Agreement on Monitoring the Management of Arms and Armies |
| BIMSTEC | Bay of Bengal Initiative for Multi-Sectoral Technical and Economic Cooperation |
| CBMs | Confidence Building Measures |
| CBRN | Chemical, Biological, Radiological or Nuclear Weapons |
| CCBLE | Civilian Capacity Building for Law Enforcement in Pakistan |
| CCIT | Comprehensive Convention on International Terrorism |
| CCOMPOSA | Coordination Committee of the Maoist Parties of South Asia |
| CFA | Ceasefire Agreement |
| CPA | Comprehensive Peace Accord |
| CPN (M) | Communist Party of Nepal (Maoist) |
| CRC | International Committee of the Red Cross |
| CrPC | Criminal Procedure Code |
| CTC | Counter-Terrorism Centre |
| CUFL | Chittagong Urea Fertiliser Limited |
| EPRLF | Eelam Peoples' Revolutionary Liberation Front |
| EU | European Union |
| FATA | Federally Administered Tribal Areas |
| HeI | Hizb-e-Islami |
| HPI | Human Poverty Index |
| HUJI | Harkat-ul-Jihadi Islami |
| HUJI-B | Harkat-ul-Jehad-al Islami Bangladesh |
| IED | Improvised Explosive Device |
| IIGs | Indian Insurgent Groups |
| IoM | Islam-o-Muslim |
| ISCN-IM | National Socialist Council of Nagaland-Isak Muivah |
| JATM | Joint Anti-Terrorism Mechanism |

| | |
|---|---|
| JI | Jamaah Islamiah |
| JMB | Jamaatul Mujahideen Bangaladesh |
| JMJB | Jagrata Muslim Janata Bangladesh |
| JTMM | Janatantrik Tarai Mukti Morcha |
| KIA | Kachin Independent Army |
| KLO | Kamatapur Liberation Organisation |
| KPK | Khyber Pakhtunkwa |
| LeJ | Lashkar-e-Jhangvi |
| LeT | Lashkar-e-Tayyeba |
| LLRC | Lessons Learnt and Reconciliation Commission |
| LOAC | Law of Armed Conflict |
| LOC | Line of Control |
| LTTE | Liberation Tigers of Tamil Eelam |
| MCCI | Maoist Communist Party of India |
| MILF | Moro Islamic Liberation Front |
| MNDF | Maldives National Defence Force |
| MNLF | Madhesi National Liberation Front |
| NDFB | National Democratic Front of Bodoland |
| NSCN | National Socialist Council of Nagaland |
| NSI | National Security Intelligence |
| PLA | People's Liberation Army |
| PPP | Pakistan People's Party |
| PPW | Protracted People's War |
| PSI | Proliferation Security Initiative |
| PWG | People's War Group |
| RAB | Rapid Action Battalion |
| RGST | Reformed General Sales Tax |
| RIM | Revolutionary International Movement |
| SAARC | South Asian Association for Regional Cooperation |
| SIMI | Student Islamic Movement of India |
| SLFP | Sri Lanka Freedom Party |
| SPA | Seven-Party Alliance |
| SSP | Sipah-e-Sahaba |
| STOMD | SAARC Terrorism Monitoring Desk |
| ULFA | United Liberation Front of Asom |
| UNLF-M | United National Liberation Front-Manipur |
| UNP | United National Party |
| UNSC | United Nations Security Council |
| VDCs | Village Development Committees |
| YCL | Young Communist League |

# *About the Contributors*

**Gen V P Malik,** who was commissioned in the Indian Army on 7 June 1959, had taken over as the Chief of Army Staff from Gen Shankar Roychowdhury on 1 October 1997. He oversaw intensified anti terrorist operations in Jammu and Kashmir and north east India, management of disputed borders with China and Pakistan and security relations with other nations. He planned, coordinated and oversaw execution of Operation Vijay to successfully defeat Pakistan's attempted intrusion in Kargil sector in 1999.

**Prof. Sukh Deo Muni** is a Visiting Senior Research Fellow at the Institute of South Asian Studies of National University of Singapore. Prof. Muni, also a Senior Visiting Scholar, Institute of Defence Studies and Analyses, New Delhi, and Editor of *Indian Foreign Affairs Journal*, superannuated from Jawaharlal Nehru University, New Delhi, India in 2006 after 33 years of teaching and research service. He also served as Professor of Political Science at Banaras Hindu University, Varanasi, India (1985-86). In 1997, he was appointed India's Ambassador to Laos and his services were again availed by the Government of India in 2005 when he was sent as a Special Envoy to Laos PDR and Cambodia to plead India's case for UN Security Council Reforms. Muni has held several visiting academic assignments abroad.

**Mr. Jehan Perera** is the Executive Director of the Sri Lankan NGO National Peace Council since 2005. Before that he has worked as the Media Director for National Peace Council (1996-2005) and Director at Sarvodaya Legal Aid Services (1988-95). He is also the secretary of the People's Action for Free and Fair Elections, a member of the Presidential Task Force on Ethnic Affairs and National Integration, and a regular political columnist on the Sri Lankan peace process for several Sri Lankan newspapers and magazines. He is the author of "From War to Peace"—a collection of articles, "Peace Process in Nagaland and Chittagong Hill Tracts: An Audit report", Co-author of "A people's Movement under Siege" and "A Manual of Civil and Political Rights" and editor of "A Gateway to Justice through Public Interest law: Proceedings of a seminar".

**Dr. Arvind Gupta** is an officer of the Indian Foreign Service (1979 batch). He presently holds the Lal Bahadur Shastri Chair in Strategic and Defence Studies at the Institute for Defence Studies and Analyses. Prior to joining IDSA, Dr. Gupta was Joint Secretary at the National Security Council Secretariat from 1999 to 2008. During his tenure at the NSCS, he dealt with a wide spectrum of national security issues. Dr. Arvind Gupta has wide-ranging diplomatic experience gained while working in Indian missions abroad. He has handled a number of assignments in the Ministry of External Affairs in different capacities. He has several books, articles and papers to his credit.

**Dr. Ashok Behuria** obtained his PhD from School of International Studies, Jawaharlal Nehru University in 1995. For his Ph.D. he worked on Ethno-communal violence as a factor in India-Pakistan relations during the Eighties using the linkage theory framework. He joined International Centre for Peace Studies (ICPS) in 1996 and worked as Assistant Director, Associate Editor of *Weekly Kashmir Trends*, Assistant Editor of *Journal of Peace Studies*. He joined IDSA in 2003 and has been working as Research Fellow on issues relating to South Asia in general and Pakistan, Sri Lanka and Nepal in particular. He has written a number of research articles, monographs and commentaries on various regional and international issues.

**Dr. P V Ramana** is a Research Fellow at the Terrorism and Internal Security Cluster of the IDSA. He is an expert on South Asian Studies, Regional Security of South Asia, Military Research and Development, Internal Security, Maoist Movements in South Asia. Dr Ramana was student of South Asian security studies. His MPhil dissertation "Role of the Navy in India's Security" (1996) and his Doctoral dissertation was entitled Military R&D in India: Programmes and Processes (2000).

**Dr. Pushpita Das** is a Associate Fellow in the Terrorism and Internal Security Cluster of the IDSA. As Research Executive in Security and Political Risk Analysis (SAPRA) between April and December 2004, she prepared a database based on various international and national newspapers, organised seminars and workshops, wrote daily reports, briefs and articles for the monthly bulletin. She has also written articles for various journals and edited books.

**Lieutenant Colonel Mohamed Ziad** assumed the duties of Principal Director of Operations at the Integrated Headquarters, Maldives National Defence

Force on 1 June 2009. Prior to this appointment Lt Col Ziad was the Commanding Officer of Support Battalion II. Lt Col Ziad's other appointments include the Chief Instructor at Girifushi Training Center, Company Commander in Special Protection Group, Deputy Commanding Officer of Special Protection Group, Deputy Commanding Officer of Rapid Reaction Force and Commander of Rapid Reaction Group.

**Dr Shivaji Felix,** an alumni of University of Colombo and the University of London, passed the final examination for the admission of Attorneys-at-Law with first class honours in 1995 and was admitted and enrolled as an Attorney-at-Law of the Supreme Court of Sri Lanka in 1996. In 1999, he was elected an Associate Fellow of the Society for Advanced Legal Studies of the University of London. In 2009 he was appointed as a Member of the Drafting Committee of the Sri Lankan National Action Plan for the Protection and Promotion of Human Rights having been appointed by the Ministry of Disaster Management and Human Rights. Dr Felix has also functioned as a consultant to the World Bank in its Country Financial Accountability Assessment Study for Sri Lanka (CFAA).

**Mr. Karma Tsering Namgyal** is Director of Bureau of Law and Order, Ministry of Home and Cultural Affairs of the Royal Government, Bhutan. He is also a member of Narcotics Control Board in Bhutan. He represented Bhutanese side in the 21st Border District Co-ordination Meeting that took place between the Royal Government of Bhutan and the state government of West Bengal, India in Thimpu on 23 October 2010.

**Mr. Deepak Thapa** is the author of "A Kingdom Under Siege-Nepal's Maoist Insurgency, 1996-2003" and the editor of "Understanding the Maoist Movement of Nepal". He has worked as a journalist for Himal South Asia and *The Nepali Times* and is currently a book editor for the Kathmandu-based Himal Books. He has also been associated with Social Science Baha, Kathmandu.

**Prof Imtiaz Ahmed** is teaching at department of international relations, University of Dhaka. His area of interest includes Political Theory, Theories of International Relations, Foreign Policy Analysis, South Asian Politics, Strategic Studies, Aid and Development, Refugee and Migration, Women and Environment, Religion and Terrorism. He has large number of publications to his credit.

**Mr Shehryar Fazli** is a Pakistan-based senior political analyst for the International Crisis Group (ICG). He first joined ICG as South Asia analyst in 2003, shortly after completing a bachelor degree in philosophy and political science at McGill University in Montreal, Quebec. In 2005 he joined the creative writing MFA program at the University of Massachusetts Amherst, where he taught undergraduate writing and completed his first novel, The Big Picture. After completing his MFA in 2008, he returned to Pakistan and rejoined ICG as Senior Analyst and South Asia Regional Editor, producing research and analytic reports on politics in Pakistan and Afghanistan. The son of a Pakistani diplomat, Shehryar has lived in various countries, including Tunisia, Morocco, Belgium, France, Mauritius, Canada and the United States.

Dr **Anand Kumar** is an Associate Fellow at the Institute for Defence Studies and Analyses (IDSA), New Delhi. After completing his PhD from School of International Studies, Jawaharlal Nehru University (JNU), he joined the IDSA in 2007. His area of specialization is Counter-terrorism, South Asian politics, Bangladesh, Maldives, Proliferation of Small Arms and Low intensity conflicts. Before joining IDSA he worked at South Asia Analysis Group on similar themes. He has also been with the Institute for Conflict Management which specializes on Counter-terrorism. He has published around 20 articles in reputed journals, contributed around 10 chapters in edited books and delivered lectures on security issues both in India and abroad. His latest article "Shaikh Hasina's Visit to India and the future of Indo-Bangladesh Relations" has been published by the Royal Society for Asia Affairs, London in their official journal *Asian Affairs*.

Mr **Chiran Jung Thapa** is currently working as a Security sector/Civil Military Relations Consultant in Kathmandu. Previously, he was employed at the Permanent Mission of Singapore to the United Nations in New York. He has worked for the World Bank/IFC in Macedonia and Institute of International Education in New York. He holds a Masters degree in International Affairs with a concentration in International Security Policy from Columbia University.

# *Introduction*

*Anand Kumar*

Today, South Asia generally evokes the image of a region that is plagued by violent religious extremism where groups like the Taliban, Al-Qaeda and Lashkar-e-Tayyeba (LeT) are active. This is also known to be a region where Maoists groups are running riot in large part of its territory. Groups like the LTTE who pursued their separatist agenda could only be wiped out with great effort. South Asia has hogged the limelight because of their activities. The phenomenon of terror has overshadowed the fact that a number of South Asian economies are growing at a fast pace and have the potential to grow even faster if not hampered by frequent acts of terror.

Terrorism has plagued the region for the last several decades. However, counter-terrorism came on to the global agenda after 9/11. Though the US has managed to thwart terror after that, South Asia has not been equally lucky. Most South Asian nations are still facing the problem of terrorism, and if anything, the problem has only intensified in several cases. Nevertheless, some positive developments have also been noticed on this front during the last one or two years which have placed South Asia at a crucial juncture where further cooperation can help the region overcome this problem.

Terrorism has defied an agreed definition. But after 9/11 there seems to be a growing opinion that this should not be allowed to come in the way of fighting a phenomenon, which is harmful to everyone. The United Nations Resolution 1390 (2002) adopted by the Security Council at its 4452nd meeting, on January 16, 2002, reaffirmed that acts of international terror constitute a threat to international peace and security.

The causes of terrorism vary from country to country. In the South Asian region, the terror groups can be placed in three categories:

1. Terrorism arising out of religious fundamentalism
2. Left-wing extremism
3. Terrorism resulting from the desire for secessionism

## Impact of Terrorism on Domestic Political Structures

Terrorism has impacted domestic political structures in South Asian countries in a negative way. It has encouraged militarism, chauvinism and a distinct tilt towards Right-wing extremism. It has been used as an excuse for undermining democracy. Though the LTTE as an organisation was set up to voice the legitimate demands of the Tamil population in Sri Lanka, its degeneration into a terrorist outfit gave the Sri Lankan state thc excuse to use brute force and follow militaristic policies and it finally succeeded in obliterating the LTTE. While this was welcomed, it also led to a massive upsurge in Sinhala nationalism, which is now coming in the way of a political settlement between the Tamil population and Sinhala-dominated Sri Lankan government.

Similar trends are seen in other states where states have boosted their military power to deal with terrorist outfits. Bhutan. which had not fought a war for centuries had to organise its military to face terrorist groups operating from its territory and also to face the likely threat from the Maoists who were very active in neighbouring Nepal. Bangladesh too had to create the Rapid Action Battalion (RAB) to face the growing threat from the Islamist radicals.

## Terrorism Hinders Economic Development

Terrorism has imposed heavy economic costs on most of the South Asian nations. The direct costs of terrorism are the destruction of infrastructure, factories and standing crops and stoppage of economic activities. Its indirect costs are varied and arise out of general loss of confidence in the economy. As a result, the economy is unable to attract foreign investment and faces brain drain, enhanced military expenditure, high transaction costs and various other economic distortions.

This is true of most South Asian countries that are affected by terrorism. Today, Pakistan and Afghanistan are in the grip of terror unleashed by Islamist radical groups including the Taliban. There has hardly been any industrial development in Afghanistan because the country has been embroiled in conflict for decades, but now even Pakistan, which was much better off compared to Afghanistan, is facing deindustrialisation in certain pockets.

## Finance: The Oxygen of Terrorism

Terrorism is generally guided by an ideology but terror cannot make much headway without finance. It is ironical that terrorism harms the economy of a country but the terrorist groups themselves require lot of money to carry out their activities. The term 'terrorist financing' is applied to two distinct but related activities. It may refer to the on-going fund-raising efforts by which a terrorist organisation supports its overall operation, arms acquisition, political activity, propaganda output, and basic training of recruits. Besides, they also need money to finance specific terrorist operations. Such transactions are equally important to compensate cadres who often put their lives at stake for the cause of the terror organisation.

Terrorists also resort to money laundering to finance their activities. Money laundering and the financing of terrorism can have devastating economic and social consequences for countries, especially those in the process of development and those with fragile financial systems. The economy, society, and ultimately the security of countries used as money-laundering platforms are all imperilled.

## The Terror Landscape in South Asia

Almost every country in South Asia is faced with the problem of terrorism—in one form or the other. Sri Lanka has successfully managed to eliminate the LTTE. However, it remains to be seen how the situation is managed by the Sri Lankan government from here on, so that no such group emerges there in future.

The situation in Nepal is also very interestingly poised. In Nepal, the Maoists were waging war against the monarchy. Now that the monarchy has been overthrown, the Maoists along with other political forces are trying to draft a Constitution for the country.

Terror has managed to mark its footprint even in the Maldives. The country has seen a rising phenomenon of Islamic extremism. There was a bomb blast in Sultan Park which left some people dead. Maldivians have fought and died in Waziristan. The problem of growing extremism has been acknowledged by none other than President Nasheed himself, who now wants to take action in consultation with his country's defence and security agencies.

Bhutan had successfully destroyed the camps of the ULFA and few other Indian Northeastern terror organisations in December 2003 but several reports now suggest that these groups are trying to regroup in Bhutanese territory. Bhutan also faces a threat from the Maoist groups who are active in both India and Nepal.

India, geographically being the largest country in South Asia, also faces major challenge from terrorism. In fact, this is one country where terrorists of all hues have been operating. Hence, it has suffered the most. For a long time, India fought its battle against terrorism alone and it has been successful to some extent. But still a lot needs to be done before this problem is properly brought under control.

In Bangladesh the government is acting against the Islamist radicals but groups like JMB and Huji still remain active. In the case of JMB the government has managed to wipe out the top leadership but the rank and file is intact. They keep throwing up new leaders from time to time. The government has however done well to capture many of them. Bangladesh also faces the problem of left-wing extremism in certain pockets but their influence seems to have been reduced in recent times.

The most serious terror threat however presently exists in Pakistan and Afghanistan. The Taliban are active in both these countries. In Pakistan they call themselves the Tehariq-e-Taliban. There are other Islamist radicals as well in Pakistan—some of whom are sectarian whereas others have an anti-India agenda.

## Beginning of Counter-terror Cooperation in South Asia

Bhutan was the first country to start the battle against terrorists. This country decided to act against Indian insurgent groups in December 2003. These groups were hiding in Bhutan and running several camps there. The king of Bhutan personally led the operation and wiped out all insurgent groups. Though this step has largely solved the problem, Bhutan still faces threats from groups who claim to be Maoists and want to dislodge the present government. This situation exists in the country despite the fact that it has successfully undergone a transition from a monarchy to a democracy.

Another interesting turnaround has been noticed in the attitude of Bangladesh. Just two days after coming to power, Sheikh Hasina declared that Bangladesh will no longer be used as a safe haven for terror, either to launch operations within Bangladesh or to use its territory to indulge in terror activities in the neighbourhood. These were not empty words. As the year unfolded, the Sheikh Hasina government took several steps which indicated its seriousness. The government adopted a two-pronged policy—it acted against Islamist groups like the JMB and the HUJI, which were creating internal disturbances within Bangladesh. It also acted against international terror groups like the LeT and the JeM. Most importantly, the Bangladesh government has acted against Indian insurgent groups.

## Failure of External Intervention in Checking Terror

The terrorist attacks of September 11, 2001 brought Western forces into South Asia. Whether they will succeed in containing terrorism or not is arguable. What is worse, even their long-term commitment is in doubt. If the economic crisis in the West worsens then it is possible that they might devise some temporary arrangement and leave the region to fend for itself.

## Regional Cooperation, the Only Way Out

South Asian countries have managed to defeat terror whenever they have cooperated with each other. Sri Lanka defeated the LTTE in a bloody war in which it received cooperation from India, Pakistan, China and some other countries.

India has managed to put insurgency in the Northeast on the back foot with the cooperation of the Sheikh Hasina government. In the past, these groups were using Bangladeshi territory to run camps and launch terror operations against India. The Bangladesh government also busted a LeT module which had members from India, Bangladesh and Pakistan. The handing over of the Indian members who hailed from Kerala, probably led to the arrest of several terror operatives in India, including top HUJI leaders who were arrested from Hyderabad. The arrests also averted terror strikes on the Indian and the US embassies in Dhaka.

The action taken by the Bangladesh government clearly revealed the wide South Asian network of extremist groups. It has also made it clear that all nations in the region must cooperate to uproot terrorism.

Unfortunately, this has not happened and ambiguity over terror persists in parts of South Asia. Some progress was made during the SAARC summit at Colombo in 2008, where leaders of South Asian countries agreed to put in place a regional legal framework to tackle the scourge. The SAARC Convention on Mutual Legal Assistance in Criminal Matters was meant to strengthen regional cooperation in the fight against cross-border crimes, specially the fight against terrorism.

The Convention calls on all member-states to provide each other the widest possible cooperation for the prevention, investigation and prosecution of crimes. The support is subject to the national laws of the states that are party to the Convention. The Convention outlines the procedure to be followed in investigations, including search and seizure, obtaining evidence, documents and witnesses in the provision of mutual legal assistance. Though the intention is positive, unfortunately the results have not been so encouraging and require a fresh look be taken at regional efforts to tackle terror.

Keeping in view the threat posed by terrorism, this book seeks to address the following questions: The problems that South Asia faces from terrorism; How have individual countries coped with terrorism; What kind of regional cooperation has taken place in South Asia; and What are the prospects of regional cooperation.

This book is based on the proceedings of the Fourth South Asia Conference, the theme of which was "The Common Challenge of Terrorism in South Asia and Prospect of Regional Cooperation." This annual conference is an endeavour of the Institute for Defence Studies and Analyses (IDSA), New Delhi, that brings together experts from all South Asian countries to discuss issues of contemporary relevance in an increasingly interdependent regional context. The theme of the first conference was "Economic Cooperation for Security & Development in South Asia" while the second conference debated the "Changing Political Context in India's Neighbourhood and Prospects of Security and Regional Cooperation". The theme for the third conference was "South Asia 2020: Towards Cooperation or Conflict?" As terrorism is an issue that concerns most South Asian nations and has held their development hostage, it was adopted as the theme for the fourth conference in 2010.

The book is divided into two sections. The first section discusses the problem of terrorism in South Asia. The second section deals with regional cooperation towards counter-terrorism.

## Problems of Terrorism in South Asia

In this section the authors analyse the phenomenon of terrorism. The experience of various countries in dealing with terrorism is also highlighted and suggestions are made for resolving the problem.

According to Gen. V. P. Malik, the former Indian army chief, terrorism is neither state-specific nor an ideology. It is a method of employing violence in the pursuit of an ideology. He finds fault with the approach that is too militarist and supports those who believe that 'ideologues' must be included in fight against terrorism. He also suggests that to defeat terrorism we should take advantage of the ideological, doctrinal and sectarian differences existing among terrorist groups. Moreover, an attempt should be made to deal with all aspects of international terrorism. A collective strategy and action plan at the regional or international level can also be devised to achieve this objective.

Prof. S. D. Muni addresses five aspects of terrorism in South Asia: the conceptual confusion; the anatomy and structure of terrorism in South Asia; its external dimensions; the responses of various South Asian states to this challenge; and policy imperatives. He feels that the events of 9/11 have had a steamrolling effect on the use and understanding of the concept of terrorism which emanates from every act of political violence. As a result, concepts and terms like 'insurgency', 'proxy-wars', 'asymmetric and unequal conflicts' have been subsumed by one word—'terrorism'. The blurring of the boundaries between the objectives and agenda of political violence and its terrorist methods reinforced by 9/11 was welcomed in South Asia, especially by the states and state supported media and analysts. He suggests that terrorism should be understood in the wider context of political violence. The root causes of political violence must be factored into crafting strategies to address the issues of terrorism and political violence.

Karma Tsering Namgyal (Bhutan) offers the perspective of Bhutan in his paper. He says that security is the top priority for Bhutan and without which Bhutan cannot achieve Gross National Happiness. He emphasises the commitment of the Royal Government of Bhutan to root out terrorism in all its forms and manifestations. Bhutan also recognises the linkages between terrorism, illegal trafficking in drugs and psychotropic substance, illegal trafficking of persons and firearms, and remains committed to address these challenges in a comprehensive manner. The government had conducted a military operation to flush out insurgent groups from Bhutanese territory in December 2003. Besides, the country has also taken a number of practical and legislative steps to implement the provisions of the Convention and the Additional Protocol since they were ratified by Bhutan.

Mohamed Ziad (Maldives) in his paper talks about preventing, and countering acts of terrorism in a small state like Maldives. In his view, present-day terrorism is not an isolated phenomenon. It has to be viewed against the backdrop of fundamental and cultural antagonisms, domestic and international politics and national and international conflicts far beyond national boundaries. It is also associated with phenomena such as radicalisation and extremism, social discrimination, economic disparities, restrictions on rights and civil liberties and power politics. He fears that the Maldives might be facing an emerging threat from extremist ideologies ranging from religious, political and social, that believe they can advance their aims by committing acts of terrorism in the Maldives.

In his paper Shivaji Felix (Sri Lanka) points out that the LTTE comprised three components—an armed group, the LTTE "network" and the "movement." Out of these three only the first one has been vanquished and it is now imperative to use diplomacy to engage the other two components and help them realise that Sri Lanka will benefit from their contribution in taking the country forward as a united nation. It is therefore of paramount importance to quell any underlying animosity by directly engaging the Tamil minority and arriving at a political settlement, irrespective of any previous military victory.

Analysing the causes of conflict in Sri Lanka, Jehan Perera (Sri Lanka) in his paper says that for the past three decades Sri Lanka was stalemated between governments that were not prepared to devolve power to the Tamil majority provinces and a Tamil militant movement that wanted nothing short of a separate country. Although the stalemate has ended with the elimination of the LTTE, significant obstacles stand in the way of a return to normalcy in the country. This is on account of the nationalist sentiments that were unleashed, on both sides, in the course of the war and which cannot be suppressed in the short term. Thus peace building and reconciliation continue to remain critical in this post-war era. The present political circumstances in the country demonstrate the need for a new paradigm of governance that is more appropriate for the pluralistic and diverse society of Sri Lanka. The centralisation and personalisation of power in governance that leads to a reliance on military force and rule by emergency decree needs to yield to decentralisation and to a rule of law-based approach to democratic governance.

Arvind Gupta, Ashok Behuria, P.V. Ramana and Pushpita Das in their paper look at the Indian experience in dealing with terrorism right since India's independence. The paper tries to identify and classify various forms of terrorism and explore how India has dealt with the menace. The paper concludes that while India has faced a variety of terror threats in the last six decades, the Indian state and society have weathered the challenge relatively well. Despite the huge loss of lives and property, terrorists have not succeeded in destabilising India or fractured its territorial and societal integrity. Part of the reason for this is the robust Indian democratic system which allows the state to employ a variety of devices ranging from negotiations to use of force to deal with numerous insurgencies and disaffections. However, the cross-border and international dimensions of the terror threat are ominous and India has not been able to deal with this aspect that effectively. Since terrorism is a global phenomenon, India needs to sharpen its diplomacy further to ensure that the external dimension of terrorism it faces is blunted. This will require a nuanced handling of its relations with Pakistan.

Deepak Thapa (Nepal) in his paper says that the restoration of democracy in Nepal following Jana Andolan II was meant to herald a New Nepal which meant different things to different people. Unfortunately, the Comprehensive Peace Accord (CPA) leading to the Interim Constitution unleashed a new phase of violence once it was made public. The paper attempts to trace some of the trends that have become apparent in this new cycle of violence in Nepal, the causes behind it and the current situation.

Imtiaz Ahmed (Bangladesh) probes the role of academics in countering terrorism. Academics are not only part of civil society engaged in reproducing social capital but also are one of the key actors when it comes to recovering, nurturing and disseminating trust, consent and tolerance in the society. He thinks that many academics have not remained true to their vocation and have started profiting from their political affiliations and have hence become indistinguishable from the coercive elements of political society or market forces. They stoop to making strategic compromises with actors and agencies with both coercive and economic powers, encouraging them in turn to contribute in many ways to the business of reproducing terrorism. Finally, he discusses various ways in which academics can help in combating terrorism.

## Regional Cooperation in Counter-terrorism

Terror groups in South Asia, have in many cases, a pan-South Asian presence. The Islamist groups or Maoists are no longer limited to one or two countries. Their ever-increasing spread necessitates that if South Asia seriously wants to contain terror, then there is no option but for the countries of the region to cooperate and take the initiative at the regional level. This is the point highlighted by authors in this section.

Shehryar Fazli (Pakistan) thinks that Pakistan-based militant groups pose the most significant threat to stability in South Asia, by their proven ability to strike at home, in India, and beyond, and with demonstrable links to international terrorist networks. The current domestic and international focus on extremist groups in the Federally Administered Tribal Areas (FATA), while understandable, has resulted in inadequate attention being focused on radical Sunni groups based in the Pakistani heartland, who are in fact, significantly more dangerous than their FATA-based counterparts. Taking credible action against them should be a top domestic and international priority. While Pakistan's elected government has pledged that it will prevent its territory from being used for attacks on foreign soil, its success in doing so will depend on political stability and a sustained democratic transition at home that enables the political leadership to wrest control of key domestic and foreign policy areas, including security and India policy; and the justice sector that has the capacity to dismantle extremist organisations and investigate and convict their members. The same challenges apply to other South Asian states, including India. He suggests that regional efforts to counter terror should build on the SAARC Convention on Mutual Legal Assistance in Criminal Matters by prioritising enhancement of civilian law enforcement and prosecution agencies, rather than current over-reliance on military action which has produced few long-term results.

Chiran Jung Thapa (Nepal) fears that South Asia can be further pummelled by terrorism. Terrorism is likely to afflict the corridor that extends from the Bay of Bengal to the western frontiers of Afghanistan spanning Bangladesh, India,

Pakistan and Afghanistan which he terms the "BIPA corridor". This region would be affected as it has almost half of the world's Muslim population where jihadi influence is increasing. The BIPA corridor has the greatest potential of becoming the foremost recruiting ground for the jihadis. SAARC efforts to deal with terrorism have failed because of the reluctance of member-states to genuinely embrace and implement the agreements. Until the SAARC member-states, particularly India and Pakistan see tangible benefits in taking on terrorism, any regional counter measure will prove to be a dud just like the Joint Anti-Terrorism Mechanism (JATM) planned between them in 2006.

Contributors to the volume consider terrorism as a phenomenon that has harmed the society, economy and polity of the South Asian nations. At the same time, they also reiterate that there should not be an over-emphasis on the use of force. In fact, a calibrated use of force is likely to be more effective. Ultimately, if terrorism is to be comprehensively defeated then the ideologies and root causes that propel it need to be tackled properly. The authors also suggest that South Asian nations must overcome their rivalry and cooperate with each other to meet the challenge of terrorism. As long as shelters and sanctuaries are available in neighbouring countries any South Asian nation would find it difficult to deal with the terror threat.

Bringing out a volume of this nature would not have been possible without the help of colleagues and friends. I would like to express my sincere thanks to Shri N.S. Sisodia, Director-General, Institute for Defence Studies and Analyses, for his encouragement and support. I would also like to convey my deep appreciation to Dr Arvind Gupta, Lal Bahadur Shastri Chair at IDSA and head of the South Asia Programme, for his encouragement at every stage which helped me to bring out this volume on time. I also sincerely thank my cluster members for their supportive role. I would also take this opportunity to thank Vivek Kaushik of the publications division. Special thanks are also due to Dr Kiran Sahni for copy-editing the text in a professional and timely manner. I would like to thank the contributors for obliging me with their updated chapters on time. I hope this volume will contribute to the understanding of the complex phenomenon of terrorism and encourage South Asian nations to cooperate so that the threat posed by terrorism is contained.

# SECTION I

# Problems of Terrorism in South Asia

# 1

# *Developing a Viable Counter-terrorism Strategy for South Asia*

*V.P. Malik*

It is a rare and lucky day in South Asia when our people are not confronted with an act of terrorism; somewhere or the other, in some form or another, for some reason or the other, terrorism ebbs and flows. It is neither definable within geographical boundaries, nor within the traditional moulds of rationality. Terrorist groups do not owe loyalty to any national flag, religion, or even ethnic community. They extinguish innocent lives as legitimate victims and often seek 'martyrdom' in suicide missions. The people of South Asia are constantly threatened by the spectre of terrorist activity. Today, there is a fear that the weapons of mass-destruction may fall into the wrong hands. It is high time, therefore, we develop a new approach to address the threat of terrorist violence in the Indian sub continent.

I would like to point out that the so called 'war on terrorism' is only a misnomer as terrorism is neither state specific nor an ideology. It is a method of employing violence in the pursuit of an ideology. The Second World War was not against the blitzkrieg, but against Nazism, which used the blitzkrieg to overrun Europe. The war on terrorism is just a mobilising term. What is required is; a comprehensive grand strategy that emphasises secular tolerance and moderation in order to win hearts and minds, while limiting the use of force to occasions where it is absolutely necessary. Implementing such a strategy will require a more holistic and coordinated approach to build up counter-terrorism capacities and partnerships across South Asia and with other stakeholders.

## Counter-terrorism in South Asia

Geopolitically, South Asia represents a unified security zone, with India at the centre. India has special ties; ethnic, cultural, historical, with each of its neighbours to a degree not shared by other states in the region. Currently, the whole of South Asia, from Afghanistan to Bangladesh, is going through a phase of internal unrest and upheaval arising from a range of destabilising factors which include ethnic conflicts, religious fundamentalism, and even intense political polarisation. The lack of political consensus and a comprehensive collective strategy necessary for capacity-building in South Asia has left the region ill equipped to tackle the terrorist threats.

Despite committing themselves to several conventions on terrorism, many states of the region continue to provide direct or indirect support and shelter to terrorist organisations. A few nations believe that someone's terrorist is someone else's freedom fighter. Such a notion is puerile as any pre-mediated and unlawful act of violence against innocent people, irrespective of the cause and motive is nothing but terrorism. Also, some nations believe that terrorism is a weapon of the small to inflict damage on the bigger nations. Such notions and advocacy reflect a lack of commitment for war against terror. My experience is that 'Terrorism is a double-edged weapon. It is like a wicked dog, which very often bites the very hand that feeds it'. India experienced it with Bhindranwale and the LTTE of Sri Lanka in the 1980s. Pakistan is realising it now, after supporting Afghan Mujahideen and outfits like Lashkar-e-Tayyeba in the 1980s and 90s.

During the November 1986 summit held in Bangalore, the heads of SAARC nations recognised the seriousness of the problem of terrorism, and its adverse impact on the security and stability of the region. Agreeing that cooperation was vital, they condemned all acts, methods and practices of terrorism as criminal, and deplored their impact on life and property, socio-economic development, political stability, regional and international peace and cooperation. The member states passed the 'SAARC Regional Convention on Suppression of Terrorism' in 1987 and agreed on several measures. An 'Additional Protocol to the SAARC Regional Convention on Suppression of Terrorism' of January 6, 2004, updated the Convention to meet the obligations devolving from the terms of Security Council Resolution 1373 (2001). In April 2007, the heads of governments once again agreed to work out modalities to implement the provisions of the SAARC conventions to combat terrorism, narcotics and psychotropic substances, trafficking in women and children, and other trans-national crimes. They strongly reiterated their commitment to take every possible measure to prevent and suppress, in particular, financing of terrorist acts, including through front organisations and also to counter illicit trafficking of narcotic drugs, trafficking in persons and illicit arms. They reiterated the need for law enforcement authorities of all member states to enhance cooperation in the prevention, suppression and prosecution of offences under these instruments. They directed SAARC interior/home ministers to ensure regular follow-up and implementation of the decisions taken.

Despite these measures, the lack of commitment to tackle the threat of terrorism has become a major concern. Nations of the South Asian region have, so far, failed to take the threat seriously and work together to tackle the transnational dimensions of the threat. The issue is crucial as cross-border terrorist activities can easily escalate into a conventional war between nations. India and Pakistan have faced such situations in 1947-48, 1965, 1971, 1999 and 2001-02. Even today, most people on both sides of the border believe that if something like the November 26, 2008, Mumbai carnage happens in India again, it could trigger a war.

It is, therefore, imperative that every nation of the sub-continent substantially raises its level of commitment and works in earnest to build trust and confidence. South Asian nations should take voluntary action against terrorist activities on their soil rather than complain, or react to each other's complaints. Governments must not be hypocritical in dealing with internationally identified cross-border terrorists, as is happening with the perpetrators of the heinous Mumbai attacks. Genuine cooperative efforts can lead to improvements, particularly in the securing of borders, disrupting terrorist financing, and restricting terrorist movements. These efforts are best undertaken at the bilateral or multilateral level, with international monitoring, where required. Experience shows that whenever terrorist groups stop enjoying state-sponsorship, they tend to whither away.

Given the lack of trust between governments in the region, there should be a greater focus on civil society and private sector actors as they can play an indispensable role in preventing terrorism. Building cooperative regional networks of civil society and private sector actors can also help build trust and the lay the groundwork for greater cooperation between states in the region.

## A New Approach/Strategy

The need for a regional strategy and cooperation is absolutely essential. At the ideological level, terrorist groups do not believe in the values of democracy, multiculturalism, and ethnic and religious tolerance. Therefore, more must be done to build and support institutional frameworks to promote these values, rather than continuing to place too much emphasis on the military approach which can easily descend into anarchy. Terrorism is not just a military problem. It is primarily a socio-political, and sometimes a socio-economic problem. A viable counter-terrorism strategy, therefore, should not only concentrate on stopping violence, but must also question and condemn irrational ideologies that undermine the development of healthy democratic institutions and good governance. For this reason, both hard power as well as soft power must be used, and calibrated, to deal with violent armed terrorists while ensuring that human rights as well as our culture and traditions are protected. An effective counter-terrorism strategy for the region should also integrate cross-cutting issues: linkages with trans-national organised crime, illicit drugs, money laundering, illegal arms trafficking, and the proliferation of nuclear, chemical and biological, and other potentially deadly materials and their means of delivery. Building capacities to counter all of these interrelated threats make sense from both the organisational as well as economic perspectives. Establishing a regional counter-terrorism centre with experts from countries of the subcontinent, who can share expertise and knowledge on a range of trans-national threats outlined above, would help. It will ensure a more seamless regional approach that could then serve as a platform for legal assistance to different countries in the region in matters relating to early investigations and prosecution.

## A Few Important Points

One, the counter-terrorism grand strategy followed in many countries with its preponderance of 'defeat, deny and defend' element is far too militarist and operationally focussed. It does not cover the ideological aspect adequately. A purely military approach, given the fragility of institutional framework in operational areas and volatility of developments, can easily descend into anarchy. I, therefore, support those who believe that 'ideologues' must be included in fight against terrorism.

Two, we need to devise collaborative strategies at the highest level. However, a uniform 'top-down strategy' cannot be applied everywhere. Counter-terrorism operational strategies and action plans should be worked out for the entire region, and in every location. It must take into cognizance the important indigenous factors to neutralise terror networks. Terrorists do have ideological, doctrinal and sectarian differences; even ego clashes arising from different cultural and national backgrounds. We need to take advantage of these differences. This can be done only if we attempt to analyse them properly.

Three, counter-terrorism strategy and cooperation should deal with all aspects of international terrorism. It should also seek a firm commitment and action to meet cross-border threats posed by the terrorists.

Four, in the counter-terrorism strategy; besides checking violence, we have to isolate and combat the ideology which is irrational and not acceptable in the modern society. We have to use all the elements of national power; not just the military but also political, economic and other kind of persuasions and pressures. Some important elements of that collective strategy and action plan would be:

1. Establishment of a 'Regional Counter-terrorism Centre' with experts from different countries who would work under a common umbrella to provide professional guidance and secretarial support to the SAARC political leadership, and monitor the implementation of their resolutions in letter and spirit.
2. Capacity building in combating terrorism of intelligence, police, military and para-military forces through training in each other's schools of instructions and thus learning from varied experiences.
3. Greater liaison and coordination for counter-terrorism operations. This would require a certain amount of inter-operability. The backbone of such inter-operability is; common inter-operable communication systems and operating procedures.
4. Updating of equipment required for counter-terrorism operations. This does not involve heavy weaponry. Rather, it requires force multipliers which enable better day and night surveillance, faster decision making and reactions, and accuracy to avoid collateral damage.
5. A common database at the regional level, a multilateral/bilateral intelligence sharing, and a mechanism for joint interrogation of terrorist leaders and key terror suspects.
6. Trust and transparency of action against sanctuaries in foreign territory and against states that sponsor terrorism. Effective action against terrorist-funding, gun running and narcotics production smuggling.
7. Legal assistance to each other in matters relating to investigations and prosecution.

## Drawing Lessons from the Indian Experience

India has been a victim of terrorism; longer than most countries, yet, it has handled the terrorist threats with some success in Mizoram, Punjab, and several other parts of the country. More importantly, it has not allowed terrorism to politically or economically destabilise the country. India has adopted a 'multi-pronged approach' and treats terrorism as a phenomenon with political, economic, social, perceptual, psychological, operational and diplomatic aspects, all of which need equal and simultaneous attention. To ensure a holistic approach, India has devised a system of unified command in terrorism-affected areas, under a governor or an elected chief minister, with committees made up of relevant government functionaries. The Indian experience with security operations in counter-terrorism has been to 'try and win the hearts and minds' of the people so that terrorists are denied moral and material support, and are thus isolated. The principle of 'use of minimum force' has guided its actions.

I would like to conclude by saying that there are no quick-fix solutions when it comes to combating terrorism. The security forces can only create conditions where the adversary is inclined or forced to come to the negotiating table. Ultimately, the solution lies in the political domain. Success requires a genuine desire and commitment to counter-terrorism which has not yet materialised among all the nations of South Asia. To address this shortcoming, South Asian governments need to enhance the level of cooperation, build trusted networks, seek the informed support of their people, providc effective governance and engage closely with the international community. Unfortunately, several vested interests within our region feel insecure and perpetuate mistrust between nations. For this reason, public awareness and interaction with civil society and the private sector become all the more important. Only then shall we be able to succeed in eliminating terrorism, prevent instability, and avoid conflicts.

# 2

# *Beyond Terrorism: Dimensions of Political Violence in South Asia*

*S.D. Muni*

Any discussion of terrorism in South Asia cannot ignore its wider influences and ramifications for the rest of the world. The issue of terrorism has been discussed by analysts and policy makers extensively from diverse and multiple perspectives, depending upon the specific context and requirement at a given point of time. In this paper, we propose to address five aspects of the question of terrorism in South Asia namely: the conceptual confusion; the anatomy and structure of terrorism in South Asia; its external dimensions; the responses of various South Asian states to this challenge; and finally, policy imperatives.

## Conceptual Confusion

Political violence and the use of terror are as old as human history. However, there has been a serious blurring of conceptual boundaries between the two since the events of September 11, 2001 (9/11), when important public buildings in the US capital city of Washington DC came under 'terrorist' attack. At times, it is asked whether raised if 9/11 was simply and solely an act of terrorism? Its answer may be sought in the targets chosen by the 'terrorists'—the symbols of US economic (World Trade Centre in New York), military (the Pentagon) and political power (The White House). The loss of thousands of innocent human lives was the result of collateral damage. However, if taking innocent American citizens was the principal objective of the attackers, then they should have chosen other targets such as the underground rail system or other crowded places. But the real target was American hegemony; the economic, military and political icons of that hegemony.

The events of 9/11 have had a steamrolling effect on the use and understanding of the concept of terrorism which emanates from every act of political violence. In this respect, the use of the concepts and terms like 'insurgency', 'proxy-wars', 'asymmetric and unequal conflicts' have been subsumed by one word, 'terrorism'. At times every and any act of public revolt that involves violence is treated as an act of terrorism, except the ruthless and indiscriminate violence unleashed by the security apparatus of a state on innocent and unarmed human beings. In reality, however, not all acts of political violence are terrorism, though all political violence may not be free from acts of terrorism. The subtle but significant difference lies in the interests, objectives, ideologies and agenda on the one hand; and methods, intensity, objects and instruments of violence on the other [1] For instance, the Tehrik-e-Taliban of Pakistan may have a larger religious and political agenda in Pakistan but their acts like the killing of university vice-chancellors in the Khyber-Pakhtoonwa province in October 2010 were indisputably the acts of terrorism. Again, an organisation like the Liberation Tigers of Tamil Eelam (LTTE) had a well articulated political goal of creating a separate state for the Tamils of Sri Lanka, but in pursuing this goal, they used ruthless and indiscriminate violence against innocent human beings. Disregarding their self proclaimed goal of liberating the Tamils, they killed a large number of Sri Lankan Tamils as well, besides others, to achieve political supremacy as a militant group. The key words officially used in most of the cases for defining terrorism are 'pre-meditated', 'politically motivated', 'non-combatants' as targets, 'sub-national groups', 'clandestine agents' etc. But all these terms are prone to subjective interpretations to suit the purpose of the user.

A balanced and objective understanding of terrorism involves a teasing out of the 'terrorist' component from the driving forces of political violence. Political violence, as generally accepted, is rooted in socio-economic anomalies and failure of governance, while terrorism seeks the cover and legitimacy from the agenda and ideology of political violence. There are however, cases and situations where terrorism snaps its umbilical cord with ideology to become a self fulfilling process, thriving upon material stakes gained through the use of indiscriminate and ruthless violence. They control commodities, they control lucrative illegal transactions and trade (drugs and arms), they indulge in abductions, killings and ransom to collect money, and they raise huge funds through charities and disaporas. The control of such resources becomes a driving force and the self fulfilling objective for terrorism.[2] Funding is a critical aspect of any insurgency movement and the access to and control of the resources leads to the abuses of the movement as was evident in the case of LTTE (Sri Lanka), Nepal Maoists, Khmer Rouge (Cambodia), FARC (Columbia) etc. But in some cases such abuses become the sole purpose of terrorist violence, as for instance in the case of Somali sea pirates.

The blurring of the boundaries between the objectives and agenda of political violence and its terrorist methods reinforced by 9/11 was welcomed in South Asia, specially by the states and state supported media and analysts. India, for instance labelled the Maoist movement of Nepal as terrorist even when the Nepal government had not done so. Subsequently, King Gyanendra sought to take the control of the state and mobilise international support in the name of fighting the terrorists i.e. the Maoist insurgency. Riding the bandwagon of 'global terrorism', many South Asian States linked their fight against global terrorism with local insurgencies to garner as much international support as possible. In Sri Lanka, President Mahinda Rajapakse's approach to the LTTE found its moral justification in the global counter-terrorism campaign of the 'international community'. After the military victory over the LTTE in May 2010, there are however very weak indications that the Sri Lankan state will pursue political resolution of the ethnic issue with the same seriousness. Pakistan, right from Gen. Musharraf to President Zardari, has been securing maximum international economic and military assistance, as well as political support, from the United States and its NATO allies for this. Much of this assistance is now being resented in sections of the US strategic community.[3]

## Anatomy and Structure of Terrorism in South Asia

Four broad categories of political violence and terrorism may be identified; ethnic/separatist; left ideological; religious/sectarian; and externally organised. All these four categories are evident in most South Asian countries. The war for a Tamil homeland by the LTTE in Sri Lanka; insurgency in the Baluchistan province of Pakistan and in India's Northeast for separate identity and statehood, all fall into the ethnic category. The Maoist movement in Nepal and the left-extremism raging in India's so called 'red-corridor' (across Maharashtra and Andhra to Orissa, Jharkhand, Chhattisgarh, West Bengal and Bihar) are the representative examples of ideologically led political violence and terrorism. In the Af-Pak region and within Pakistan, jihadi terrorism driven by Islamic extremism and aimed at promoting a 'purist' Islamic state, is being confronted by the 'international community, in collaboration with Pakistan and Afghanistan. There has now also been an official acknowledgement of 'saffron' or 'Hindutva terrorism' in India.

Lastly, there is 'cross-border' terrorism against India inspired and organised by Pakistan. This cross-border terrorism goes beyond fuelling political unrest in

India's Jammu & Kashmir to reinforce Pakistani claims on this region, and extends to whole of India with the purpose of weakening its economy and sabotaging its political and social stability. The latest disclosures with regard to the Mumbai terror attacks in November 2008 clearly reveal the character of externally organised terrorism in South Asia. Analysts also point out that India's involvement in the Tamil insurgency in its early stages, or Bangladesh's support and sheltering of India's Northeast insurgents or China's support for the first phase of Naxal insurgency in India during the late sixties and early seventies also can be taken as examples of externally organised political violence and terrorism in South Asia. It can be no doubt, but the critical difference between all these examples and that of the Pakistani 'cross-border' terrorism against India is that all the former cases of political violence had their basic roots within the country of their manifestations and the neighbours exploited the turmoil and conflicts for limited strategic and foreign policy goals. What Pakistan has done in Mumbai and at many other places in India is a category in itself, wherein terrorism is used as a systematic instrument of strategic policy, of confronting and weakening India; of waging a war by other means.

The above categories however are not rigid. There is considerable overlap and spill-over among them. Take for instance, the extremist left ideological groups; the Maoists; in India and Nepal. The ethnic component in these insurgencies is clearly visible. The Nepal Maoists mobilised the marginalised ethnic groups like Magars, Gurungs, Limbus, Kirats, Thakalis, Tamangs etc. This has added the powerful agenda of meeting the aspirations of these 'nationalities' to the ideological programme of the Maoists. In case of Indian Maoists, the tribals from the backward eastern region are the mainstay of the insurgency. There are also other regional identities enmeshed in the movement that are reflected even at the leadership levels and in the strategies being pursued by the insurgents. Similarly, in the predominantly Tamil ethnic insurgency of Sri Lanka, various militant groups were divided along ideological lines. The Eelam Peoples' Revolutionary Liberation Front (EPRLF) with its strong Marxist orientation had a perpetual ideological discord with the LTTE. Even with the religion driven terrorist groups with allegiance to Islamic extremism, sectarian (Shia-Sunni) and ethnic divisions cannot be ignored.[4]

Besides the ethnic and ideological overlap in the categories of insurgent and terrorist groups in South Asia, the groups also have logistic and ideological supportive linkages, even across the borders. The LTTE in Sri Lanka consistently tried to link up with Indian and other insurgent groups to promote their commercial interests (selling arms and explosives, providing training etc.) as also to forge a common front against the Indian atate. Reports of the LTTE's links with the Andhra Maoist groups and Northeast ethnic insurgents have appeared in Indian media. The Nepali Maoist leader Prachanda also confessed that the LTTE had approached them for mutual support but the Maoists did not accept the offer.[5] The nature and extent of ideological and logistic linkages between the Nepal Maoists and the Indian left-extremist groups have been debated in the Indian media for a very long time.[6] The South Asian Maoists groups forged an institutional relationship in July 2001 by establishing a Coordination Committee of the Maoist Parties of South Asia (CCOMPOSA). This committee meets periodically and adopts resolutions in support of 'revolutionary struggles' in South Asia. Also the terrorist outfits in India like Indian Mujahedeen's are suspected to have linkages with jihadi groups in Pakistan and even Al Qaeda. The links between Al Qaeda and the Pakistani Taliban and jihadi groups are well established.[7]

There is a tendency among the policy makers and political leaders to project the terrorist and insurgent groups as coherent organisations. This is far from the ground-reality of these groups. The diverse and differentiated natures of these organisations become evident, on closer scrutiny of their various layers and tiers. The constituencies that extend social and political support to them constitute different groups who have suffered displacement, exploitation, discrimination and mis-governance. Issues directly affecting them range from denial of land, threats to their living patterns and cultural identity, access and traditional rights over forests and caste and religious prejudices etc. They are genuinely interested in improving their living standards and protecting their life styles. In terms of the objectives and commitments, there are generally variations at three broad levels: leadership, militant cadres and social support constituencies. The leadership is from the upper sections of the social strata and is educated urbanised and has greater exposure. None of the insurgent groups have been free from leadership rivalries driven by power ambitions and ideological differences.[8] They are motivated by political objectives of attaining power and shaping governance and society. The militant cadres join the movement for different objectives. Not more than five per cent of those who pick up the gun and indulge in violence are believed to be motivated by the stated ideological objectives of the movement. Most of them do so to overcome hardship and deprivation, to make quick money, to settle personal scores with their local adversaries, or the sheer thrill of wielding a gun and dominating others. A number of women cadres join these movements to over come gender discrimination and family exploitation/ violence. The Nepal Maoists and the LTTE had a sizeable strength of women cadres; up to 30 per cent or more. This is in sharp contrast to jihadi terrorist who may use women as suicide bombers but do not enrol them as active cadres.

On the parameters of organisational cohesion, ethnic and ideological insurgencies have been more compact than others. The LTTE was perhaps one of the world's most regimented terrorist group. Its cyanide culture (the cadres carrying a cyanide capsule to be swallowed in the case of arrest) made it extremely secretive and with Prabhakaran, the supreme leader dominating, it was run on fascist lines. The Maoists of Nepal and India also have little transparency about their organisational functioning, but their structure is federal as they draw their support from various regions and diverse communities, castes and ethnic groups. The most dispersed and locally autonomous of the South Asia terrorist groups are the Al Qaeda and the jihadi outfits. The Al Qaeda is broadly understood to be a hydra-headed sprawling organisation with an uncoordinated network. The counter-terrorism analyst Leah Farrel recently described it as:

> Al Qaeda today is not a traditional hierarchical terrorism organisation, with a pyramid-style organisational structure, and it does not exercise full command and control over its braches and franchises. But nor is its role limited to broad ideological influence. Due to its dispersed structure, al Qaeda operates as a developed network hierarchy, in which levels of command authority are not always clear; personal ties between militants carry weight and, at times transcend the command structure between core, braches and franchises.[9]

Some of the jihadi organisations based in Pakistan but operating at the global level have been influenced by Al Qaeda in their organisational structures and methods of functioning. Some of them like Lashkar-e-Tayyeba and Hizbul-Mujahideen have also assumed a humanitarian façade by undertaking relief and resettlement work in the events of natural calamities like floods and earthquakes. The Maoists of Nepal and India, as well as the LTTE also had front organisations to help them mobilise popular support, raise funds and propagate their agenda. Such support goes beyond national boundaries, and is related to the external dimension of South Asian political violence.

## External Dimension

The external dimension of terrorism in South Asia comprises the trans-national ideological and identity linkages of the terrorist and insurgent organisations as well as the policies and approaches of the countries around, towards them. The Maoists of India and Nepal have obviously been inspired by the ideologies rooted outside these countries and they have established strong linkages with groups and organisations that are have similar ideologies. The Nepal Maoists were strongly influenced by the Peruvian communist rebels and had organisational links with the Maoists of the world, including with the Revolutionary Communist

Party of America. The Nepali and Indian Maoists became the active members of the Revolutionary International Movement (RIM) which has committed itself to encouraging and supporting extremist communist groups all over the world with the proclaimed aim of transforming political and socio-economic systems through revolution. At the regional level, the Maoists groups of South Asia have organised themselves through CCOMPOSA since 2001 as noted earlier. These ideological links have been helping insurgents groups in various ways, from recasting and sharpening their ideological positions to exposing them to diverse contexts of 'revolutionary struggles' being waged in various countries. The Nepal Maoists, for instance adopted 'Prachanda Path' (derived from the Maoist chief Prachanda) a local version of their ideological agenda just as the Peruvian rebels had adopted 'Shining Path'. Besides ideological reinforcement, the trans-national linkages among the Maoists have helped them in propagating their cause and in mobilising political support and even financial resources. It has also facilitated their armed training and acquisition of arms and explosives.

The South Asian insurgencies have their identity linkages at two levels: with the persons belonging to other countries but of the same identity and with their compatriots settled in other countries as the diaspora. The ethnic identity between the Tamils of Sri Lanka and India, or between the Nagas of India and Myanmar or between the Nepalese of Nepal and India may be seen as the examples of the first and those between the LTTE and the Tamil diaspora, and the Nepal Maoists and the Nepali diaspora, or the Al Qaeda and Taliban with radicalised Muslim masses all over the world may be seen as the examples of the second. Cross border identity linkages have provided strong support to the insurgent groups in the legitimacy of their cause (for instance the small but aggressive support among Indian Tamils for the cause of Tamil Eelam in Sri Lanka), as also in other offering shelter, training, mobilising funds and logistic support for the families of the fighting cadres. The diaspora support has been a strong source of funding and international advocacy. Some details of this aspect have been discussed elsewhere with regard to the Nepali Maoists and the LTTE.[10] There is considerable literature on the funding of Al Qaeda and jihadi groups through cultural organisations, business establishments and voluntary contributions in Muslim countries.[11]

It is important to note here that while insurgent groups and terrorists have been able to operate their external linkages more efficiently and effectively, cooperation among the South Asian states affected by terrorism has been rather poor and disappointing. All most all South Asian countries are guilty of supporting terrorism in their neighbouring countries at some stage or the other. India supported Tamil militancy in its early stages during the 1980s, due to internal pressures as well as to help protect India's then perceived strategic interests in the region from Sri Lankan government's counter-terrorism approach of involving extra-regional powers.[12] The Nepali Maoists also sought support and shelter in India with or without the knowledge and support of the Indian government. The Indian insurgents, particularly from the Northeast region and Jammu & Kashmir, have also been seeking shelter and support in Pakistan, Bangladesh, Myanmar and Bhutan. We have already mentioned Pakistan's cross-border support for terrorism against India and Afghanistan.

With the exception of Pakistan, however, in all other instances, the terrorism supporting countries have withdrawn such support.[13] India's war against the Tamil tigers, through the Indian Peace Keeping Force from 1987 to 1990 may be seen as in atonement of its earlier 'sins'. Some of India's neighbours like Bhutan and Myanmar have been cooperating in the fight against insurgents. For the past couple of years since the coming to power of the present Awami League regime in Dhaka, Bangladesh also has committed itself to helping India fight the Northeast insurgencies and jihadi terrorists. But Pakistan continues to see an advantage in supporting, if not all, at least the chosen jihadi outfights, as instruments of its strategic policy towards India and Afghanistan which has constrained SAARC from fighting terrorism collectively at the regional level, despite its longstanding commitment to do so since 1987.[14]

Terrorism and insurgencies are a global phenomenon and the dynamics of world politics impinge upon it in many decisive ways. During the Cold War period the great powers used the insurgent groups as instruments to settle strategic and ideological scores with their adversaries. Support for communist insurgencies by the then Soviet Union and China in many countries of the developing world and the counter use of coups and rebellions by the US, were described in scholarly literature as 'proxy-wars' waged by the great powers against each other. In the post-Cold War period, the utility of such proxy wars remains though their quality and contexts have been radically altered. The shift in the global power structure is also seen as a factor in the changing character of insurgencies and terrorism.[15]

Since 9/11, a stronger tendency on the part of the South Asian states to depend upon external support for fighting internal insurgencies and terrorism has become evident. In this respect, while the US has emerged as a significant ally in fight against terrorism in Afghanistan, Pakistan, Nepal and India, a critical role was played by China, Russia, Pakistan and India to help Sri Lanka inflict the death blow to the LTTE militarily in 2009. The US and its European allies' involvement in fighting terrorism in South Asia emanates from the threat posed to these countries by Al Qaeda and Islamic extremists with roots in Pakistan and Afghanistan. There is however a subtle and critical distinction being made by the West, approach in South Asia, between 'global terrorism' that directly affects them (mostly Islamic extremism) and 'local terrorism' that poses a challenge only to South Asian countries. Consequently, the support extended by the US and its European allies to the South Asian countries in fighting terrorism is carefully calibrated. Accordingly, the US treats 'global terrorist' outfits like Al Qaeda and Taliban differently from what they consider to be 'local terrorist' groups like, the Indian Maoists, Indian Mujahedeen, Kashmiri militants or the LTTE. The increasing internal security threats have also opened up large markets for Western security gadgets, small arms, training and intelligence services and counter-terrorism ideas and literature.

## State Responses

No single South Asian pattern of state response to the challenge of political violence and terrorism can be identified or should even be expected. Most of the state responses have been reactive rather than preventive or pro-active. In all these responses, the use of force has been a pre-dominant feature where unplanned, excessive and indiscriminate force has been used by the state agencies. This has proved to be counter-productive, often helping the insurgent groups to widen their social support base and reinforce their recruitment and commitment to violence. The war of liberation waged by Sri Lanka in 1987, Nepal's operations of 'Romeo' and 'Kilo-Sierra-2' during the late nineties, the first phase of police operations in the Punjab in India during the early eighties and also India's recent initiatives like Salwa Judum and 'Green Hunt' against the left-extremism may be recalled.[16] Pakistan has been fighting a war of differing intensity with the Al Qaeda and Taliban extremists without much success. The only one case of an outright military victory against insurgency in South Asia was recorded by Sri Lanka in May 2009, though some in India like K.P.S. Gill claimed that the Punjab insurgency was overcome through well-planned police operations.[17]

Notwithstanding the primary reliance on use of force, there is a growing realisation among the South Asian states that the challenge of political violence is a complex one and it cannot be met by the use of force alone. The criticality of the political, constitutional and governance aspects of political violence are now being realised and the states are gradually factoring in these aspects in their respective strategies of counter-terrorism and conflict resolution.[18] But there are still innumerable issues of coordination, proper use of force in view of mounting human rights concerns, political patronage of selective insurgent constituencies for electoral purposes, etc. that make the task of state authorities difficult and challenging. In a federal country like India, political disharmony between the central and the state administrations adds to the complexity of coordination among security forces and law and order machineries. The states are becoming more sensitive and responsive to the interventions of the civil society groups while dealing with insurgencies and terrorism.

There are two conflict resolution models for ending political violence and terrorism that have emerged in South Asia till date. They will continue to influence South Asian approaches in the years to come. In Nepal where the Maoist insurgents decided formally in 2005 to join the mainstream and work towards their agenda through peaceful and democratic means in cooperation with other democratic parties. India also played a significant role in facilitating the transition in the Maoist line from the 'peoples' war' to a peaceful resolution. In some ways India also, at least partially succeeded in resolving the insurgency issue to some extent through political accommodation in the Northeast. The other model is of Sri Lanka where the state under the leadership of President Mahinda Rajapakse decided to eliminate the LTTE through a full scale war and succeeded in doing so in May 2009. Both these models are not perfectly successful as yet. While the Maoists continue to harp upon 'revolutionary methods' and their mainstreaming is far from accomplished, in Sri Lanka, not many are hopeful that an amicable political solution of the ethnic issue will emerge under President Rajapakse. The United Nations and the international community continue to cry foul over the gross violations of human rights during the last phases of Sri Lanka's war against the LTTE.[19]

South Asian states are also becoming conscious of the value of mutual cooperation, at least at the bilateral level, in dealing with the challenge of terrorism. The contiguous boundaries and ethnic identities have made the neighbouring countries realise that the spill over of political violence and strategic use of terrorism have a boomerang effect in the long run. India took nearly six years to persuade Bhutan to extend such bilateral cooperation in 2003 in dealing with the Bodo and ULFA insurgents of India who were using Bhutan's southern Duars (forested flatlands) as sanctuaries. India's shift in its approach towards the Myanmar military junta also facilitated bilateral cooperation from 1995 onwards, in dealing with the insurgent spill over between the two countries. We have already noted the cooperation between India and Sri Lanka as also between India and Bangladesh in this respect. There is now much better intelligence coordination and exchanges between these countries on terrorism related issues. However, in the absence of any basic change in Pakistan's position it would be unrealistic to expect any viable regional approach to emerge within or outside the SAARC or the BIMSTEC (Bay of Bengal Initiative for Multi-Sectoral Technical and Economic Cooperation) frameworks. Extra-regional powers and international organisations like UN (including UNSC resolutions on countering terrorism), Interpol, are helpful in the overall fight against terrorism, but they have not, and perhaps cannot, play a decisive role in South Asia.

## Policy Imperatives

The foregoing discussion on the question of political violence and terrorism in South Asia leads us to the following policy imperatives.

1. Terrorism should be understood in the wider context of political violence. The root causes of political violence must be factored into crafting strategies to address the issues of terrorism and political violence.
2. Strategies of fighting terrorism and resolving the issues of political violence need to be comprehensive and balanced. Use of force can be a part of such strategies but not the sole instrument. Also the use of force has to be carefully calibrated and well planned. Indiscriminate and excessive use of force must be shunned at all times. Considerable emphasis has to be accorded to constitutional, political and socio-economic accommodation of alienated groups in conflict resolution strategies. This may slow down progress but would prove to be effective and lasting in the long run. It would help if the anatomy of terrorism and insurgent groups is carefully mapped out, and differing ethnic loyalties, cultural clusters and motivations are identified among leadership, cadres and social constituencies while evolving counter-terrorism strategies. Civil society groups may play a meaningful role in facilitating a comprehensive strategy evolved by state agencies.
3. South Asian countries have not yet adequately and systematically explored the strategies of reconciliation, reintegration, accommodation and mainstreaming in relation to the insurgents and terrorist groups. The insurgent and terrorist groups use 'cease-fire', 'engagement' and 'negotiations', as tactical gestures to improve their bargaining positions and even gain time for pursuing their agenda of violence and terror. That should not dishearten the state agencies.
4. The core challenge of counter-terrorism lies at the national level. International organisations, including the UN, extra-regional forces including the most powerful ones like the US and China may be helpful, but only up to a limit. They cannot play a decisive role.
5. The most-effective way to deal with cross-border terrorism is through bilateral cooperation.

## NOTES

1. For discussion of some of the issues involved, see Roberta Senechal de la Roche (Ed), "Theories of Terrorism: A Symposium", in *Sociological Theory*, Vol.22, No.1, March, 2004. For a discussion of terrorism from the perspective of counter-terrorism, see, Boan Ganor, "Defining Terrorism: Is One Man's Terrorist Another man's Freedom Fighter?", in *Police Practice and Research,* Routledge, Vol.3, No.4, 2002, pp.287-304.
2. There is considerable literature on the funding and financing of the terrorist groups. For some reference here, see, Costigan,S. and D. Gold, *Terrornomics*, Ashagate Publishing, Hampshire Burlington, 2007. Passas, N. "Commodities and Terrorist financing: Focus on Diamonds", *European Journal on Criminal Policy and Research,* Vol. 12, No. 1, 2006, pp.1-33. Levitt, M. "The Political Economy of Middle East Terrorism", *Middle East Review of International Affairs Journal,* Vol.6, No. 4, 2002.
3. David Sanger and Eric Schmitt, "White House Assails Pakistan Efforts on Militants", *New York Times,* 06 April, 2011, http://www.nytimes.com/2011/04/06/world/asia/06pakistan.html.
4. Muhammad Amir Rana, *A to Z of Jehadi Organisations in Pakistan*, Mashal Books, Lahore, 2004. Imtiaz Gul, *The Al Qaeda Connection: The Taliban and Terror in Pakistan's Tribal Areas*, Penguin Books India, New Delhi, 2009. (See Appendix 2 and 3).
5. See his speech at Observer research Foundation on November 18, 2006. *ORF Discourse,* Vol.1,No.3. December, 07, 2006.
6. P.V. Ramana, "Linkages between Indian and Nepali Maoists", IDSA Comment, http://www.idsa.in/idsacomments/LinkagesbetweenIndianandNepaleseMaoists_pvramana....
7. See Rana, *op.cit.*, and Gul, *op.cit.* Also see, Ahmed Rashid, *Descent Into Chaos,* Allen Lane, London, 2008.
8. See for example on Tamil Tigers, Narayan Swamy, N.R. *Tigers of Lanka: from Boys to Guerrillas*, Konark, New Delhi, 2002, also his, *Inside an Ellusive Mind: Prabhakaran*, Little World Publishers, New Delhi, 2003. Prashant Jha, "Maoists in Nepal: the differences within", *The Hindu* December 07, 2010.
9. Leah Rarrall, "How al Qaeda Works", *Foreign Affairs,* Vol. 90, No.2, March/April 2011, pp.128-138. Also see, Rohan Gunaratna, *Inside Al Qaeda: Global Network of Terror*, C. Hurts & Company, London, 2002.
10. S.D. Muni, "Globalisation and South Asian Insurgencies", in George Heine & Ramesh Thakur (Editors), *The Dark Side of Globalisation*, United Nations University Press, Tokyo, New York, Paris, 2011, pp. 123-143.
11. Rachel Ehrenfeld, *Funding Evil: how terrorism is financed and how to stop it*, Bonus Books, 2003; Burr. J & Collins. R, *Alms of Jihad: Charity and Terrorism in the Islamic World*, Cambridge University Press, New York, 2006; Jeaune K. Giraldo and Harold A. Trinkunas (Edited), *The Political Economy of Terrorism Finance and State Responses: A Comparative Perspective*, Stanford University Press, 2006. Also see Pravin Swami, "Diaspora Cash fed domestic Jehad", *The Hindu*, May08, 2009.
12. See, S.D. Muni, *Pangs of Proximity: India and Sri Lanka's Ethnic Conflict*, Sage Publications, 1993. Also, Rohan Gunaratne, *Indian Intervention in Sri Lanka: The Role of Intelligence Agencies*, South Asian Network on Conflict resolution, Colombo 1993.
13. The latest criticism of Pakistan for its laxity in dealing with terrorist groups is in the European Parliament condemning Pakistan saying that "elements of the Pakistani intelligence and security services are suspected of giving practical and financial support to terrorist groups". The Times of India, April 16, 2011.
14. Sridhar K. Khatri, "Fighting Terrorism Through SAARC?", in S.D. Muni (Edited),

*Emerging Dimensions of SAARC*, Foundation Books, Cambridge University Press-India, New Delhi, 2010.

15. Ajai Sahni, "Terrorism and the Global Power Shift", A paper presented at the conference on "Terrorism in South and Southeast Asia in the Coming Decade", June 26-27, 2008, Institute of Southeast Asian Studies, Singapore.
16. For some of the details, see, S.D. Muni (Ed.) *Responding to Terrorism in South Asia*, Manohar Publishers & Distributors, New Delhi, 2006.
17. K.P.S. Gill, "Endgame in Punjab; 1988-1993", *Faultlines: Writings on Conflict & Resolution"*, vol.1, ICM-Bulwark Books, May 1999.
18. See for details, S.D. Muni, *Responding to Terrorism in South Asia, op. cit.*
19. See for instance the report of the UN Advisory panel appoint by the Secretary general on Sri Lanka which has brought out "credible allegations" that the Sri Lankan State committed war crimes and offences against humanity. *The Independent* (London), April 17, 2011.

# 3

# *Lessons Learnt and Future Prospects in Post-war Sri Lanka*

*Jehan Perera*

Sri Lanka has a pluralistic society composed of several different ethnic communities, the two largest being Sinhalese and Tamil which have characteristics of nations. The centralised state inherited by the newly independent country in 1948 effectively transferred political power into the hands of the Sinhalese majority who comprise about three fourths of the population. The inability of the political elites belonging to the different ethnic communities to share power equitably among themselves led to a series of broken agreements and to acute mistrust between the communities. The difficulty of protecting minority interests in a unitary system of government in which majority-minority relations are strained is exemplified by Sri Lanka's modern political history. As the Tamils from the north in particular were rarely represented in the higher rungs of the government, they were unable to influence the government into taking their concerns into account. The inability of Tamil politicians to obtain adequate redress for their grievances eventually led to the build up of separatist sentiment, militancy and war.

For the past three decades Sri Lanka was stalemated between governments that were not prepared to devolve power to the Tamil majority provinces and a Tamil militant movement that wanted nothing short of a separate country. In February 2002, the Sri Lankan government and LTTE signed a ceasefire agreement under Norwegian government auspices that appeared to offer the real prospect of a final end to violence as a means of conflict resolution. The ceasefire between the government and the LTTE held for nearly four years despite significant problems affecting the peace process; problems that led to the LTTE's withdrawal from the peace talks. However, the ceasefire collapsed in early 2006 with a series of ambushes of government soldiers by the LTTE, eventually leading to counter measures and counter attacks by government forces in which the government wrested back the territory placed under the control of the LTTE as per the terms of the ceasefire agreement. The Sri Lankan government's defeat of the LTTE, which became the main Tamil separatist and armed movement, and the destruction of its command and control structures, presents an opportunity for political and economic progress in Sri Lanka.

The last phase of the war was one of the most challenging in the annals of modern warfare. This ensured that the Sri Lankan war hogged the headlines in the international media. The LTTE in its retreat herded the Tamil population of the northern territories it once, controlled on to a tiny patch of land. Using more that quarter of a million civilians as human shields they sought to keep the Sri Lankan military forces at bay, and buy time for to ensure their continued survival. Virtually unanimously, the international community urged restraint, the non-use of heavy weapons that could cause indiscriminate casualties, and the evacuation of the civilian population. But a very large number of civilians, in the tens of thousands, are believed to have either died or been injured in the fighting that ensued.

Although the stalemate has ended with the elimination of the LTTE, significant obstacles stand in the way of a return to normalcy in the country. This is on account of the nationalist sentiments that were unleashed, on both sides, in the course of the war and which cannot be suppressed in the short term. The militarily victorious Sri Lankan government now faces the challenge of promoting reconciliation and lasting peace in Sri Lanka. It needs to obtain international support to supplement its own resources for rehabilitation of displaced persons and the victims of war and in putting the country on the fast track of economic development. The government will also require international cooperation in preventing sections of the Tamil diaspora who have for long supported the violent activities of the LTTE from seeking to keep the fires of hatred burning in Sri Lanka through acts of internationally sponsored terrorism. In addition, there is a need to learn lessons from the past conflict, make peace and not repeat the mistakes of the past.

## Lessons Learnt from Failure of Peace Process and its Aftermath

### *Agreed Parameters*

Given the fears, suspicions, expectations and positions taken by the government and LTTE, it was important that the parameters of the final settlement be agreed to at the outset, or if not at the outset, at some time at the beginning of the peace process. These parameters ought to have included the unity and indivisibility of the country which the international community as a whole supported in principle. This was in the minds of those who supported the ceasefire agreement and the peace process, but it was evidently not in the mind of the LTTE. This was obvious from their interim proposals for an interim self-governing authority, which appeared to be a half way house to a separate state.

### *Bipartisan Consensus*

The Bandaranaike-Chelvanayakam Pact of 1957 was the first attempt at a negotiated settlement of the ethnic conflict. This and all succeeding attempts failed, in part, due to an inability of the government and opposition parties to reach a bipartisan agreement on the envisaged political reforms. The ceasefire agreement and the political negotiations between the government and LTTE proved to be no exception. The government that signed the agreement and attempted to negotiate with the LTTE did so without the support of the opposition. The government was also internally divided on the issue, with the prime minister and his government not receiving the support of the president of the republic who was kept out of the process by the government. As ethnic conflict is an emotive issue imbued with primordial fears, there is a necessity for a broad government-opposition consensus for a solution to be developed.

### *Public Participation*

In a democratic society it is important that the electorate and the population at large be apprised of political developments that matter to them. The issues need to be explained and the consent of the people needs to be obtained. The government had pledged to arrive at a ceasefire in its election manifesto. But once the peace process commenced it did not adequately inform the people about the dilemmas it was facing and neither did it take them into confidence about the hard choices it had to make. This task was largely left to civil society and NGOs, which was insufficient as the government has much more power to reach a mass audience.

### *Human Rights Violations*

Human rights violations took place during the period of the ceasefire agreement. In particular, the LTTE assassinated its political rivals, government intelligence operatives and embarked on large scale recruitment—including child recruitment—during this period. Many national and international organisations concerned with peace were cautious in highlighting these violations on the grounds that this might induce the LTTE to withdraw from the peace process and re-start the war that had ended and which had already led to the loss of tens of thousands of lives. The return to war was not seen as an option by those who supported the peace process, and the emphasis was on averting a return to war. It was important that human rights be protected in full, and not in part, at every stage of the peace process from beginning to end, which did not happen.

### *Restricted Information*

The necessity to fight the war was widely accepted, not only in Sri Lanka but also internationally. However, the human costs of the fighting and the fact that hardly any independent information was available lead to an international backlash. Both the international media and international humanitarian organisations only had very limited access to the war zones. As a result it was difficult to obtain independent verification of what was happening in the war zones and the casualties. This may account for international human rights groups and the UN secretary general taking a focused interest in the last days of the war.

### *Political Solution*

The government set up an all party representatives committee that met continuously during this period and submitted a final report to the president. However, during the last phase of the war, this report dropped out of sight. Attention was focused on the impending military victory, after which it was made to seem as if the entire problem was over. But a military solution did not eliminate the political roots of ethnic conflict. Now that the impediment of the LTTE is absent, there is a renewed opportunity for a negotiated political solution with the elected representatives of the ethnic minorities. The absence of such a political solution has allowed the critics of the government to assert that the ethnic conflict continues and that the government is not interested in the peace, justice and reconciliation that should accompany a political solution.

### *Post-war Phase*

During the last phase of the war it became evident that there would be an influx of internally displaced persons. The government announced that it was setting aside land and putting up shelters to temporarily accommodate these people. But enough was not done. When the 300,000 displaced persons crossed over into government-controlled areas, they had very little by way of planned and organised facilities to house them. Being well preparing for these people would have demonstrated that the government was concerned about their welfare and was conducting, along with the war, a humanitarian operation on equal scale on their behalf. This needs to be redressed today by the rapid provision of permanent housing, infrastructure and livelihood.

### *NGO Access*

There are still tens of thousands of displaced persons who remain in camps, in temporary shelters and with relatives in various parts of the North and also some parts of the East. Women and children are in a particularly vulnerable situation. There are many women-headed households amongst the war victims. At present many of the resettled people have been sent back to totally devastated and virtually jungle-like areas to fend for themselves with hardly any resources. While army personnel are assisting the people in their resettlement efforts, they have few resources and need more. There are still about 8000 LTTE cadre who are to be reintegrated into society. NGOs have specialised competencies in the areas of rebuilding communities and reintegrating ex-combatants into civilian life. Restrictions placed on the work of non-governmental organisations which have human and material resources need to be minimised.

### *Demilitarisation*

There is presently very close involvement of the military in the life of the civilian population in the North and East where the military continues to play a role in governance. The fact that the military is engaged in civilian activities may be because the government desires to utilise the excess manpower for constructive purposes now that the war is ended. However, this should be a temporary arrangement pending the re-establishment of civil administration. In addition, the ethnic composition of the security forces needs to reflect the ethnic pluralism in society.

### *Peace Education*

One of the challenges to national integration and reconciliation will be to give people from different ethnic communities a better understanding of those from other communities. The stance of politicians from rival camps tends to get replicated at the grassroots, furthering the divide and promoting ethnically polarised voting patterns. The work of politically non-partisan civic groups is important to heal the wounds created by the bid for political power. They should be encouraged not stymied by various government imposed restrictions. There needs to be greater trust between government authorities and the civic groups working for peace and reconciliation through dialogue and not only regulation.

## Security Focus

Despite the end of the war the government has not relaxed its grip on security. Defence allocations in the budget have increased, not decreased, and the country continues to be governed under the emergency law which gives the security forces additional powers. In the government's second budget after the end of the war the defence appropriation of Rs 215 billion dwarfs the resettlement appropriation of Rs 1.7 billion. It also dwarfs the second largest component of the budget which is economic development which got Rs 75 billion. This was so in the last budget as well when Rs 201 billion was allocated for defence versus Rs 3 billion for resettlement and the same amount being allocated for economic development about the same. The budget appropriation bill demonstrates that the government's priorities continue to be defence and national security.

When the security of the state takes priority over the welfare of the people the outcome is a national security state. On the occasion of the previous budget, the government sought to explain the disparity between the budget allocations for defence and other ministries by citing the continuing security needs of the country. They said that the government was establishing new police stations and other security posts in the former war zones of the North and East. Such efforts are clearly visible along the roads to which the ordinary traveller has access, and are also reported to be underway in the interior by those who are allowed access to the areas or live there. On the occasion of the present budget the government's rationale for the extraordinary—and continuing—rise in the already high defence expenditure was the salary bill for the 500,000-strong security forces including the police and payment of instalments for the military hardware bought during the war.

Concerns over a possible resurrection of Tamil militancy is likely to be a key determinant of the government's security policy for the foreseeable future. The possible resurrection of LTTE remnants is also likely to determine the government's policy on the resettlement of displaced persons. Due to international pressure the government has completed most of the resettlement. However, vast tracts of land taken over by the military as "high security zones" remain in their control although the original rationale no longer exists in the absence of the LTTE and its long range artillery. Instead of demilitarising the Tamil majority areas of the North and East, the military occupation is being consolidated by the building of new military bases with living quarters for families of the military. All of this sends a message of mistrust and alienation to the civilian population.

Underlying the government's emphasis on security issues is the strong Sinhalese nationalist component in the present Sri Lankan government. This nationalist support was crucial to the government in politically sustaining the war effort despite its high cost. Having collaborated with Sinhalese nationalism it will be difficult for the government to abruptly reverse itself and seek new political allies. Nevertheless if a break with the past is to be obtained, it is necessary that the government should learn from the lessons of the past and not repeat them.

In the longer term any government is bound to pay a price with dissatisfaction rising within the general population due to economic hardships. This is particularly true of the Tamil population, which suffered tremendously during the years of the war. They will be particularly critical of a government misallocation of resources that marginalizes their urgent concerns of reconstruction, resettlement and rehabilitation. But it is also true of the general population who are unlikely to be much impressed by government claims of macro economic growth figures of 8 per cent plus, or by a booming stockmarket to which the masses of people have little or no access. Such economic progress will be merely a concept to the majority of people who see a progressive deterioration in their purchasing power on a daily basis.

It may be in anticipation of a potentially restive population that the government is continuing to beef up the security forces with new recruitment instead of de-militarisation after the war. New military installations are visible in the North and there are reports that the government is also planning to set up similar installations in other parts of the country also. This suggests a strategy of having the military as a back up to civilian authority in the governance of the country. In the former war zones of the north and east, the military often plays the lead role in governance and substitutes for the civilian administration which has crumbled by years of displacement by the LTTE and other Tamil militant organisations. However, there also appears to be an anticipation of a future usefulness of the military to quell situations that go beyond the control of the civilian administration in other parts of the country as well.

The unwillingness of the government to repeal the Prevention of Terrorism Act and also the continued validation of Emergency Rule by Parliament on a monthly basis is difficult to understand as a necessity more than a year and a half after the end of the war and the elimination of the LTTE, which the government has celebrated on many occasions. The continuation of governance under Emergency Law which was first imposed to cope with the growing insurgency now appears to have become the norm, with Parliament routinely voting to keep the government armed with these extraordinary powers of repression. The availability of repressive laws and a powerful military machine would send a message to the larger society of a potentially repressive climate of governance. The danger of having emergency and anti-terrorist laws is that they will be used as a first resort rather than as a last resort by a government that relies on a strong military to maintain law and order.

## Restoring Confidence

At the same time, as the government moves to address its own concerns regarding ethnic separatism and how best to contain it, the government also needs to reassure the ethnic minorities that their own concerns will be addressed. The recent history of Tamil separatism and the LTTE's war to achieve an independent state of Tamil Eelam, would justify the government's concerns about devolving power to large units such as the provinces. On the other hand, if the government is to treat the ethnic minorities on an equal footing and as equal citizens, it needs to address their aspiration to be politically empowered in the areas in which they live.

Restoring the confidence of the Tamil people in the government would be the major challenge in the forthcoming period. The heavy human costs in the last phase of the war have generated anxiety and uncertainty amongst the Tamil population. Despite being victimised by the LTTE, who forcibly taxed and recruited from amongst the Tamil population, and finally held the civilian population hostage in the war zone, many if not most Tamils viewed the LTTE as a force capable of extracting necessary concessions from the Sri Lankan government.

An immediate measure that needs to be given priority attention would be to ensure that the displaced civilians are provided with improved relief and rehabilitation services, and are resettled in their home villages as soon as possible. Those who are displaced and are being resettled continue to be very poor and vulnerable in an environment that continues to be highly militarised. The government's expectation is that economic development will empower the people. The problem is that the government's preparations for resettling the people have been so limited. Now it is as if they are being literally dumped into the middle of jungles. Although the Indian government and other donors have promised to provide resources for house building and other infrastructure that benefits the people, the progress on the ground is very slow due to governmental inaction to allocate the land and to give the name lists of the beneficiary families. This could also be indicative of the reluctance of the Sri Lankan government to permit foreign entities into those areas for security reasons.

A stark feature of the proposed government budget is the vast disparity between the amount committed to defence and to resettlement. The government's explanation for the very small allocation of Rs 1.7 billion for resettlement is that nearly all of the war displaced persons have been resettled, and only about 20,000 still need to be resettled. The reality however is that physically taking back people to their previous locations where they lived is not resettlement. When people are taken back and put into the midst of land in which all buildings and infrastructure is destroyed, and the jungle has grown, it is not resettlement where the government can wash its hands, and say that it has done its duty, and now the people must fend for themselves. It is indeed tragic that the government is prepared to devote so much of resources to satisfy the needs of its defence budget and so little to satisfy its war displaced people.

An explanation for the small allocation from the government's budget to resettlement could be that the government expects the international community to make donations and provide for the war displaced people. If this is the case, then the government will need to urge the international donors to make their commitments for the sake of the war displaced persons. In this context, the front page photograph in the Sunday Times newspaper that showed an official of the International Committee of the Red Cross breaking down and weeping while on a visit to the North to hand over such international aid is not likely to be encouraging to the international community. The news item that accompanied the photograph stated that the ICRC was providing 400 tractors to war affected people who had been pre-selected, but a government minister had given those tractors to a different set of people. The government will need to subscribe to certain norms and standards if it is to continue to receive international support.

Another confidence building measure would be to ensure the physical and mental security of Tamil citizens living throughout the country. During the period of the war there was a breakdown of law and order in which a spate of kidnappings, murders and extortions targeting Tamil people in particular occurred in all parts of the country, especially in Colombo and the north and east. The government empowered paramilitary groups and special units within the security forces to take action against LTTE members and active sympathisers. Over the past three years several thousands of Tamils are reported to have been abducted and many of them have disappeared. There are no reliable statistics as the government denies any role in these abductions and has been very critical of independent organisations that attempted to compile such figures.

## Emphasising Centralisation

The government has also shown its intention of further centralising power with

Parliament approving the $18^{th}$ Amendment to the Constitution by the 2/3 majority necessary for constitutional change. The $18^{th}$ Amendment took away checks and balances necessary for good governance and restraint on the abuse of power. It removed the term limitation on the Presidency, which had limited any incumbent to two terms of six years each. The $18^{th}$ Amendment also gave back to the President the power to appoint a plethora of powerful state officials. The government has justified the constitutional change as being necessary for the political stability that will generate economic development.

The government has justified its actions on the basis that it ensures stability in government policy which is necessary for rapid economic development to take place in the aftermath of the protracted civil war. Macro economic statistics bear out the assertion that Sri Lanka is on the road to economic boom. The second quarter of 2010 saw economic growth reach up to 8.5 per cent, up from 7.1 per cent in the first quarter and much above the 3.5 per cent figure for 2009. The coming into production of arable land in the Northern and Eastern provinces which were most affected by the war, and the opening up of the seas has also led to a boost in production. Reflecting the improved economic prospects, the stock market has appreciated by over 100 per cent in the past year.

As a politician known for his pragmatism, President Rajapaksa is likely to conform to the views of his government's nationalist allies. His disavowal of Western political categories and rejection of the concept of minorities has met with overt Sinhalese approval. The President's reference to a home grown political solution and his disavowal of foreign models in his address to Parliament suggests that the devolution of power to the provinces will not be given priority. Instead it suggests that the government will follow the model already explicated in the case of the Eastern Province. The Eastern Province development model is one in which the government held local and provincial elections in the newly cleared areas in alliance with former Tamil militants who joined up with it against the LTTE. Those elected are then built up as a new Tamil leadership with which the government does business in terms of economic development, but without further political concessions that improve the devolution of power.

The government appears to hold to the belief that rapid economic development of the country, including the North and East, would productively engage the energies of people and reduce the impetus towards ethnic-based politics. However, such an analysis is not in keeping with international experience. The values and symbols of the ethnic majority if imposed upon the ethnic minorities in an environment of populist nationalism can aggravate conflict. Ethnic-based grievances and desire for self-determination exists in both rich and poor countries which economic development by itself cannot dispel. Tibet in

China and Chechnya in Russia give ample testimony to the resolve of aggrieved ethnic minorities to seek some form of regional self-government above all other values.

Government members have said that further constitutional reforms will be coming in sequence. Future reforms are likely to include changing the electoral system from being one based on proportional representation to one that has mixed elements of both the first-past-the-post system and the proportional system. This is already taking place with regard to local government with the concurrence of the government and the largest opposition party, and over the objections of the ethnic minority and small political parties which will be disadvantaged by these changes. Another likely reform would be in regard to the 13th Amendment which established the devolution of powers through provincial councils as the solution to the ethnic conflict. There are elements of the 13th Amendment that have been controversial since its passage in 1987.

The provincial council system has been criticised from two opposing perspectives. Some believe that the devolution of powers to the Provincial Councils is an effective way to ensure a measure of power sharing between the ethnic communities. As the Northern and Eastern provinces in particular have a majority who comprise Tamil and Muslim voters, devolving powers to those Provincial Councils enables the ethnic minorities to wield those devolved political power within those provinces. But the supporters of the provincial council system are disappointed at the lack of resources provided to them and to the lack of implementation of important sections of the law.

Others however have been critical of the Provincial Council system as providing too much of power them that could be used for anti-national purposes. The critics point to the power over land and police in particular, as these can be used by the Provincial Councils to promote separatism. They have argued that if the Tamil militant movement was able to become so powerful without the provincial councils being vested with those powers, it can be imagined how much more powerful any rebel movement would be if they had access to land and police powers as well. This apprehension has led to successive governments denying police and land powers to the Provincial Councils.

Now that the government has obtained for itself a 2/3 majority to change the constitution, it can be expected to move swiftly to remove police and land powers from the list of powers that the 13th Amendment assigned to the Provincial Councils or in the alternative will reduce those powers. The issue of police and land powers has always been controversial with the ethnic majority Sinhalese population being fearful that such powers could be utilised to further strengthen and entrench separatist sentiment. As a possible sop or trade off, the government may come up with an upper house of Parliament whose representation is drawn from the provinces, but in which the ethnic minorities will remain a minority. The government would be encouraged by the ease with which it was able to pass the 18th Amendment. Amending the 13th Amendment would be even easier as it has been controversial with large sections of the population. Such a constitutional amendment would also change hardly anything on the ground. As in the case of the 17th Amendment that was overridden by the 18th Amendment, it would merely make formal what had previously been the practice.

In conclusion, it can be seen that although the open conflict has ceased, the divisions that existed in the past are still very much alive. The violence, suspicion, and segregation of the conflict have become deeply embedded in social and political life. The differences that exist between communities are mobilised by political leaders to further communal agendas. The economic progress taking place in the country can be threatened by instability due to the increased political polarisation. Thus peace building and reconciliation continue to remain as critical needs in this post-war era. The present political circumstances in the country demonstrate the need for a new paradigm of governance that is more appropriate for the plural and diverse society in Sri Lanka. The centralisation and personalisation of power in governance that leads to a reliance on military force and rule by emergency decree needs to yield to decentralisation and to a rule of law-based approach to democratic governance.

# 4

# *India's Experience in Dealing with Terrorism*

*Arvind Gupta, Ashok Behuria, P.V. Ramana and Pushpita Das*

> Our country has been a victim of terrorism for the past more than two decades. Terrorism has been used as a means to destroy the values on which our nation is built. Terrorist groups enjoy patronage and sanctuaries and do not lack in resources. We therefore have to ensure that our capabilities to combat terrorism remain a step ahead of those of the terrorists. They should be left in no doubt whatsoever about our ability and resolve to defeat them.
>
> —*Dr Manmohan Singh, Prime Minister of India, Valedictory Address at the Golden Jubilee Celebrations of National Defence College, October 22, 2010, New Delhi*

This paper surveys the Indian experience of dealing with terrorism ever since independence. It tries to identify and classify various forms of terrorism and explore how India has dealt with the menace. Broadly, there are four types of terrorism that have been threatening the Indian state since independence: terrorism in Kashmir and Punjab sponsored by Pakistan; identity-related ethnic conflicts in the Northeast: left-wing extremism and Islamic radicalism connected to global jihad that also has a cross-border dimension. The main conclusion of the paper is that while India has faced a variety of terror threats over the last six decades, the Indian state and society have weathered the challenge relatively well. Despite the huge loss of lives and property, terrorists have not succeeded in destabilising India or affecting its territorial and societal integrity. Part of the reason for this is the robust democratic system which allows the state to employ a variety of devices, ranging from negotiations to use of force, to deal with numerous insurgencies and disaffections. However, the cross-border and international dimensions of the terror threat are ominous and India has not been able to deal with them as effectively. Much more needs to be done to improve India's counter-terrorism strategies.

## Various Studies

There is a large body of literature on terrorism in Asia and South Asia in general and India in particular. The studies, on India, have focussed on the roots of terrorism,[1] the nature and form of terrorism, the strategies India has adopted to counter terror[2] and the emerging challenges for the Indian state—given its rather soft approach to terrorism.[3] The literature available on various violent conflicts within India is also quite substantial. These works have analysed the triggering factors, the underlying causes and the dynamics that have sustained the violent movements for autonomy, secession and independence in states of Jammu and Kashmir and some states in the Northeast.[4] Several arguments are thrown up by these studies. There is a view that because of India's hesitant response to terror,[5] it is a "sort of laboratory where major acts of terror are first tried out before being replicated in the democracies of the West". Some others have appreciated the way India has dealt with the issues related to terrorism.[6] India has used its constitutional mechanism, as well as force very prudently and judiciously and largely succeeded in handling such threats. There are some studies on terrorism and political violence in India which argue that poverty, underdevelopment, social cleavages and competitive party politics create conditions for growth of terrorism in India.[7] The studies on the emerging jihadi threat in India refer to the cross-border connections of the "internal mujahideen" and recommend better and stronger internal security practices. They argue that India needs better counter-intelligence, coordination amongst security forces and cooperation with international agencies to counter this menace.[8] While these are important there is also a need for a comprehensive study of the various terrorist threats faced by India, analyse their causes, and assess the Indian approach to them—which is what this paper attempts to do.

## The Indian Experience with Terrorism

India has been facing terrorism—defined here as political violence designed to spread panic, and in which non-combatants are targeted[9]—right since its inception in 1947. Over independent India's 63 years of history, terrorism has been used by militants, insurgents and even criminal gangs against India. During these years, India has largely dealt with terrorism more as a law and order problem than as an independent phenomenon in itself. However, an effort is made here to identify the various forms of terrorism faced by India over the years.

## Externally sponsored

The tribal invasion of Kashmir, aided and assisted by Pakistani forces, was the first instance of state-sponsored terrorism against India to wrest Kashmir. It was a demonstration of the use of terrorism by a state as a tool to achieve foreign and security objectives. Thousands of infiltrators sent by Pakistan into Jammu and Kashmir in 1965, which precipitated the Indo-Pak war of 1965 was yet another instance of state sponsored terrorism. The trend continued in the late 1980s when Khalistani militants were assisted by Pakistani forces to launch a full blown insurgency in Punjab. In the late eighties and nineties, Jihadi groups based in Pakistan supported Kashmiri insurgency and employed terrorism as a tool in Kashmir to intimidate the India state.[10] The terrorist attack on the Indian Parliament (2001), the numerous terrorist attacks (2001-2008) throughout India including the Mumbai terrorist attacks in November 2008 (26/11) are attributed to Pakistan based Lashkar-e-Tayyeba, Jaish-e-Mohammad, Harkat-ul-Mujahideen and other such groups. These groups are linked to Al Qaeda and have developed global ambitions. Some other groups like Harkat-ul-Jihadi Islami (HUJI) from Bangladesh have also participated in various terrorist attacks throughout India. The territories of neighbouring counties have been used for launching many of these attacks. India has also been the victim of the terrorist attacks made by the Liberation Tigers of Tamil Eelam (LTTE) in the past, losing Indian Prime Minister Rajiv Gandhi to one such attack in 1991.

## Ethnicity and Identity-related

India has also seen numerous indigenous insurgencies in the Northeast, where groups like United Liberation Front of Assam (ULFA), various factions of National Socialist Council of Nagaland (NSCN), National Democratic Front of Bodoland (NDFB) etc. have used terrorist methods as well as external support in furtherance of their objectives of secessionism and separatism. Many of these insurgencies have either been controlled or are waning but some of them are continuing.

## Left-wing

India is currently facing a serious left wing insurgency spearheaded by the Maoists in central and eastern India. This insurgency is fuelled by the left wing ideology of overthrowing the state through an armed revolution and establishing an alternate system of governance based. The long list of left-wing uprisings in the country includes the Telengana Armed Struggle (1948-51), the Naxalbari movement of the 1960s and the Srikakulam Armed Struggle (1968).[11] The first phase of the present-day pan-India Maoist insurgency commenced with the tribal-peasant uprising, in 1967, in the Naxalbari village of the then Siliguri sub-division of West Bengal. In its current phase, the insurgency began with the founding of the Communist Party of India—Marxist-Leninist (People's War), PW in short, popularly known as People's War Group (PWG), in 1980, by Kondapalli Seetharamaiah, a school teacher, in Karimnagar district of Andhra Pradesh. An Indian home ministry acknowledges the presence of several left-wing extremist groups "in certain parts of the country for a few decades now."[12] Some of them have now become defunct, while others remain active. Of these, the most lethal is the Communist Party of India (Maoist), which was founded on September 21, 2004, by the amalgamation of the PW and the Maoist Communist Party of India (MCCI). In fact, the CPI) (Maoist) has been responsible "for more than 90 per cent of total left-wing extremist incidents and 95 per cent of resultant killings", during 1999-2010.[13] The following tables illustrate the profile of Maoist violence in the country since 2005.

**Table 1: Fatalities in Maoist Violence, 2005-09**

| | 2005 | 2006 | 2007 | 2008 | 2009 |
|---|---|---|---|---|---|
| Andhra Pradesh | 208 | 47 | 33 | 82 | 18 |
| Bihar | 96 | 45 | 53 | 88 | 72 |
| Chhattisgarh | 168 | 388 | 311 | 320 | 290 |
| Jharkhand | 119 | 124 | 123 | 256 | 208 |
| Madhya Pradesh | 3 | 1 | 2 | 1 | - |
| Maharashtra | 53 | 42 | 22 | 31 | 93 |
| Orissa | 14 | 9 | 16 | 109 | 67 |
| Uttar Pradesh | 1 | 5 | 3 | 1 | 2 |
| West Bengal | 7 | 17 | 3 | 26 | 158 |
| Kerala | 0 | 0 | 0 | 0 | - |
| Karnataka | 8 | 0 | 5 | 7 | - |

**Source:** Ministry of Home Affairs, *Annual Report*, various years, New Delhi.

The Maoist ideologues have cleverly exploited the shortcomings in governance and failures of the state in providing justice, development and security to mobilise the poorer populations in various parts of the country. Some of the issues raised by the naxals, i.e. the issues of land rights, exploitation by contractors and corrupt officials, displacement etc., resonate with several sections of Indian civil society. On the other hand, there is a complete disconnect between the reasons for cadres

**Table 2: Maoist Violence Profile, 2010**

| State | 2010 (January 1 to July 15) | | | | |
|---|---|---|---|---|---|
| | No. of Incidents | Civilians Killed | Security Forces Killed | Naxalites Killed | Naxalites Arrested |
| Andhra Pradesh | 46 | 7 | 0 | 7 | 165 |
| Bihar | 174 | 40 | 5 | 4 | 218 |
| Chhattisgarh | 357 | 88 | 144 | 50 | 402 |
| Jharkhand | 279 | 70 | 12 | 9 | 206 |
| Madhya Pradesh | 6 | 0 | 0 | 0 | 0 |
| Maharashtra | 43 | 10 | 2 | 2 | 33 |
| Orissa | 119 | 29 | 16 | 1 | 85 |
| Uttar Pradesh | 4 | 1 | 0 | 0 | 75 |
| West Bengal | 203 | 117 | 32 | 28 | 257 |
| Others | 1 | 0 | 0 | 1 | 42 |
| Total | 1235 | 362 | 211 | 102 | 1483 |

**Source:** Statement Referred to in Reply to Parts (a) and (b) of Lok Sabha Starred Question No. 23, "Naxal Attacks", July 27, 2010, New Delhi: Lok Sabha Secretariat.

joining these underground groups and the objectives of the leadership. People join the ranks of the CPI (Maoist) either because the issues raised by the group resonate with their own aspirations or for personal reasons, while the ultimate objective of the leadership is the 'capture of political power' through a protracted people's war (PPW). On the other hand, there have also been reports of fraternal linkages between the Indian Maoists and the Communist Party of Nepal (Maoist).

## Jihadi and Reactive Religious Extremism

There is a fourth strand of terrorist groups who champion global jihad for establishing an Islamic Caliphate. The long email sent to Indian media by a shadowy group called "Indian mujahideen" minutes before Ahmedabad serial blasts in July 2008 outlined the jihadi agenda of the Islamic Mujahideen in great detail.[14] In the recent past, many terror attacks in India have been linked to this group (Indian Mujahideen) and the Student Islamic Movement of India (SIMI). The demolition of the Babri masjid in 1991 and the Gujarat communal riots in 2002 gave a fillip to the growth of jihadi groups, as well as right wing extremist groups related to fringe outfits championing a militant version of Hinduism.[15] This is a relatively new phenomenon in India whose import is not fully appreciated. The indigenous religious terror groups with linkages abroad have added a new dimension to the terror threat faced by India.

## India's Vulnerabilities

The question that needs to be asked is why has India been the target of these terror attacks and how has it dealt with terrorism? And has its approach been successful?

There are two broad reasons for this; these are not the root causes but they are sufficiently strong explanations. The first one is Pakistan's implacable animosity towards India right since the partition of the sub-continent on the basis of the two-nation theory. The inexorable logic of this theory led Pakistan to eventually become an Islamic state. In contrast, India, preserving the pluralistic, multi-lingual, multi-religious character of its society, chose the secular and democratic path. Pakistan's quest for parity with India embroiled it in a constant state of hostility with India. After 1971, following the birth of Bangladesh, a dismembered Pakistan became even more antagonistic towards India. It did not hesitate to use terrorism as a tool of its foreign policy. This is evident in the case of Pakistan sponsored and supported militancy in Punjab, terrorism in Kashmir, and jihad in India.

Apart from Pakistan, China also supported insurgencies in India's Northeast until 1979 at least. Many of India's insurgent groups have taken shelter in Myanmar, Bangladesh and Bhutan in the past. India has found it easier to deal with the insurgencies whenever its neighbours have cooperated with it—Bhutan in 2004, Myanmar (ongoing) and Bangladesh (during the current tenure of Prime Minster Sheikh Hasina). Thus, the external dimension in indigenous insurgencies has always been paramount.

Second, India's diversity is both its strength and a weakness. In a pluralistic and democratic society, dissatisfied groups and individuals find it relatively easier to exploit the societal fault lines and the inability of the state to provide justice, equality, development and good governance. They have greater degree of manoeuvrability in an open society and they have exploited this freedom to the maximum.

Even though terrorism has been a long standing problem in India and the violence has been of high order, it can be argued that India has by and large managed its terrorism problems relatively well. Terrorism has not succeeded in changing the basic character of India, i.e., democracy, pluralism and tolerance despite considerable loss of life and property. In many cases, insurgencies have either been won over or attenuated. However, terrorism continues to pose a serious national security threat to India. The threat is likely to grow in the future as the global linkages of the terrorists deepen. Continued failure on the governance front will also make it difficult to deal with indigenous insurgencies.

## India's Response

The most striking aspect of India's response to terrorism has been its effort to deal with such menace within the framework of India's democratic constitution. India has a liberal Constitution which grants fundamental rights to its citizens. These rights are justiciable. In addition, the Indian constitution also guarantees special rights to its religious and ethnic minorities. The Indian Constitution has numerous provisions designed to accommodate aspirations of diverse groups. While dealing with terrorism, India has sought to deal with the reasons underlying the numerous insurgencies.

A number of insurgencies in India are based on the assertion of ethnic and regional identities. The Indian Constitution has innovative provisions to accommodate the aspirations of ethnic and regional groups. It provides for setting up of regional councils with varying degrees of autonomy. This device has been used successfully to deal with insurgencies in the Northeast. Article 370 of the Indian Constitution, although a "transitory provision", provides for a special status for the state of Jammu and Kashmir (J&K). There are similar provisions for some states in the Northeast. J&K is the only state in India to have its own constitution.

The holding of elections on a regular basis, the constitutional arrangements on the sharing of power between the centre and the states, the all-India civil service, the election commission and judiciary have helped foster national integration and a sense of Indian nationalism. Over the years, the Indian state has also devolved greater financial resources to the states. In the 1990s, the Constitution was amended to give greater powers to the Panchayats—the governing units at the village level. The Indian state has also used reservations in public employment, political and social institutions to grant social and economic rights to the deprived groups through affirmative action. More and more women are thus being brought in to local political structures. As a result of these factors, very often, the insurgent movements, which employ terror as a tool, lose public support as in the case of United Liberation Front of Assam (ULFA). Once a popular movement, it rapidly lost public support in 2004 when it killed 18 innocent children in a bomb blast at Dhemaji. The militancy in Punjab also became unpopular when violence began to be used indiscriminately against innocent people. There is also a feeling that the Naxal movement may also have plateaued as it is becoming increasingly brutal. Loss of popular support and the resultant weakening of insurgencies create the ground for mainstreaming them through a process of dialogue and power sharing.

**Table 3. Handling Terror: The Indian Way**

| Area | Type and other details | Measures taken to handle the issue |
|---|---|---|
| Jammu & Kashmir | Externally sponsored. Sustained by state agencies. | Constitutional provision (Art 370)<br>Dialogue with local leadership<br>(Beg-Parthasarathy talks, Indira-Abdullah accord, Rajiv-Farooq Abdullah understanding)<br>Talks with secessionists<br>Autonomy measures |
| Punjab | Identity related and externally sponsored<br>Call for separate homeland | Strong internal security measures<br>Dialogue with Pakistan<br>Accommodation of demands |
| North East<br>(7.7% of territory, 3.745% of population) | Autonomist and Secessionist<br>(Assam, Arunachal Pradesh, Manipur, Meghalaya, Mizoram, Nagaland and Tripura)<br>In some cases foreign hand has been there | Dialogue (peace talks) with political leadership<br>CR efforts succeeded in Meghalaya, Mizoram and Arunachal Pradesh<br>Talks with Naga rebels on (70 rounds of talks)<br>Talks with ULFA unsuccessful (but top leadership in Bangladesh). No move to abjure violence. |
| Central, Eastern and Southern India | Naxal Movement<br>Left-wing Extremism<br>13 of 29 states<br>165 out of 602 districts | Invitation for unconditional talks<br>Internal security measures |
| Spread through out India | Jihadi terror<br>External hand quite discernible | Legal and coercive measures |

## Use of Force

Despite these measures, the Indian state has continued to face insurgencies, some of which take to terrorism, to press home their points of view. When the existing mechanisms do not work, the Indian state has not hesitated to use force in a determined manner to deal with political violence. The use of force is often necessary but indiscriminate use leads to greater radicalisation.

The Indian armed and paramilitary forces try to use force in a restrained and calibrated manner. They have not used aerial bombardment or heavy artillery against insurgents or terrorists except—briefly—against the Mizos in the 1960s. As a result, the Indian forces have taken heavy casualties in their fight against insurgencies. However, they have constantly adapted their strategies to the counter the changing tactics of different terrorist groups and insurgents. In recent years, the armed forces have also been sensitised to human rights issues.

While the state has the monopoly over the use of force, there are practical limitations on its effectiveness. The state some times uses force in a haphazard and ad hoc manner. Excessive use of force can also be counter-productive as the movements get radicalised. The prolonged use of force brings into question the credibility of the state. In addition, indiscriminate use of force can have adverse socio-economic consequences. The local populations also feel alienated. It is, therefore, important that the force is employed in a "well-planned calibrated manner."[16]

## Legal Measures

Fear of violent retribution by terrorist groups inhibits people, including the victims themselves, from assisting the police and the judiciary in prosecuting the terrorists. In a number of cases, they might not even want to lodge a complaint in a police station. Thus, there is no gainsaying that it is an uphill task for the police and the prosecution to obtain conviction against terrorists. To an extent, some judicial officers, too, might fear being neutralised by the terrorists. Hence, there is a possibility that they might grant them bail or discharge them in a case. Thus, a senior advocate of the Supreme Court of India, who prosecuted terrorists in Punjab argues that:

> [t]he reasonableness of the procedure and mechanism for preventing and coping with terrorist offences must, therefore, be judged keeping in view the evil with which the law has to contend, the circumstances under which the evil is to be dealt with, the kind of parties before the court, and the mental condition of the witnesses. The law, therefore, has to balance the liberty of an individual with that of other, and with the requirements of the security of State, and the sovereignty and integrity of the nation.[17]

Over time, India has enacted a number of legislations to deal with the menace of terrorism. However, the enactment of a specific and dedicated anti-terror law and its implementation and/or abuse, has always been politically contentious, leading to vacillation in the government's approach. Nevertheless, the Indian state has always emphasised the non-violability of the Rule of Law in dealing with terrorists. A list of legislations employed by India to deal with the terrorists and terrorist activities, which lays down the broad legal frame-work of India's response to terrorism is given in Annexure I.

## International Cooperation

International cooperation has been an important part of India's counter-terrorism effort. Presently, India is signatory to all the major anti-terrorism conventions of the UN. It has also proposed a Comprehensive Convention on International Terrorism (CCIT). It abides by the numerous UNSC resolutions like 1373 and 1540 in dealing with terrorism, particularly, WMD terrorism. India has cooperated in some initiatives like the container security initiative and the recently launched nuclear security initiative although it has reservations with regard to associating itself with the US-sponsored Proliferation Security Initiative (PSI).

India has been at the forefront of the fight against international terrorism. After 9/11, international opinion turned against movements employing terrorism as a tool even if the causes they championed had wide sympathy. Thus, LTTE lost international support after 9/11. This was a major factor in its ultimate defeat at the hands of the Sri Lankan army. China stopped supporting Indian insurgents in the Northeast in the late seventies. This helped in the weakening of many of these movements. On the bilateral level, India has received help in countering terrorism from Bhutan, Bangladesh, Myanmar, Sri Lanka and Afghanistan. The SAARC Convention on terrorism is an important instrument in fight against terrorism. However, cooperation amongst South Asian countries in dealing with terrorism is sub-optimal. In comparison, India has received useful help from the US and the Western countries in responding to terrorism by way of information sharing and capacity building. The intentional dimension will remain an important factor in India's struggle against terrorism.

Speaking at the 34th Munich Conference on Security in 2002, the then National Security Advisor of India noted emphatically and correctly[18]:

> The world now accepts that terrorism can be tackled effectively only with a global and comprehensive approach. UN Security Council Resolution 1373 shows the right direction. However, the world's democracies have to co-operate effectively in its implementation and ensure compliance of other countries. This requires collective political will, undiluted by short-

> term political or economic calculations. Whatever our political predilections or strategic calculations, we cannot condone terrorism somewhere, while condemning it elsewhere, because this lenience will boomerang on all of us. We have to systematically choke off the three crucial lifelines of terrorist groups: refuge, finances and arms.

International cooperation suffers from many drawbacks. The coordination amongst countries on intelligence sharing, capacity building and joint action is sensitive and politicised. The lack of an agreement over the definition of terrorism/ terrorist groups also comes in the way of international cooperation. The absence of extradition treaties hampers cooperation in dealing with terrorist incidents. India has faced the problem of cross border terrorism for several decades but the cooperation of neighbouring countries in this case has not been satisfactory. The international community lacks the means to deal with the states sponsoring terrorism. Despite the efforts made by Financial Action Task Force, the flow of funds to terrorists has not been stemmed.

## Shortcomings

Despite these measures, there is a great deal of public unhappiness with India's counter-terrorism efforts. The dissatisfaction has increased particularly since the 26/11 Mumbai attacks, compelling the government to take some measures to strengthen India's counter-terrorism machinery. The key weaknesses in India's counter-terrorism efforts have over the years, been identified as: the failure of intelligence, lack of coordination amongst numerous security agencies, weak laws, failure to prosecute terrorists, ill-trained police, lack of equipments, etc.

However, the most serious deficiency appears to be the lack of political will in dealing with terrorism. India does not have an accepted definition of terrorism nor does it have a counter-terrorism doctrine. This is in sharp contrast to coherent strategies followed by such groups as LeT or the Naxals. India's responses are mostly judged to be ad-hoc and tactical even though a vast amount of resources have been spent on combating terrorism.

A few examples can be cited. The government did not appear to have a proper strategy to deal with the aftermath of the terrorist attacks on the Indian Parliament. It ended up mobilising practically the entire Indian army (Operation Parakram) on the borders for several months. This resulted in considerable attrition for the Indian armed forces which remained on full alert for several months without any clear objectives.

The 26/11 Mumbai attacks showed that India had not done enough to prevent terrorist attacks launched from outside the country. The Indian coast turned out to be highly vulnerable to terror attacks. Even though India has long experience of dealing with terrorism, there was a remarkable lack of coordination among agencies in dealing with the terrorist attack which continued for nearly sixty hours. The role of the media in covering the attacks was also questionable. The media ended up helping the terrorists and prolonging the duration of the attack. More important, the government did not quite know how to deal with Pakistan from whose soil these attacks were launched and whose agencies had collaborated with the LeT in launching these attacks. The 26/11 attacks seriously derailed Indo-Pak relations which have not yet been normalised. Moreover, the public still does not know how the government will react if a 26/11 type of terrorist attack occurs again in the future.

The nuclear factor has imposed constraints on the Indian government to deal with sub-conventional attacks emanating from the Pakistani soil. An additional complicating factor is the distinct possibility of non-state actors including the jihadi groups getting access to nuclear and radiological material.

The 26/11 Mumbai attacks exposed the vulnerabilities of the Indian coast. The responsibility for maritime security is diffused and spread over dozens of central and state agencies which makes coordination difficult. The law dealing with maritime security is also weak and inadequate. The Indian navy now regularly escorts Indian and foreign ships in the Gulf of Aden, protecting them from Somali pirates. Thus, the Indian navy as well as the Indian coast guard have been called upon to deal with terrorist attacks that can be launched from the sea.

The biggest problem remains developing proper counter-terrorism capabilities. It has become increasingly clear that India is in the crying need of judicial and police reforms in order to deal with terrorist threats. In addition, India needs to improve the quality of governance. Inclusive economic growth, the new *mantra*, is required but even more necessary is the need to ensure that people get justice and the delivery of services takes place without harassment or corruption. The political system in the country also requires cleaning up through electoral reform and strict action against corrupt politicians and officers.

Terrorists are increasingly using the modern technologies like the Internet, social networking sites, satellites and cell phones and appear to be ahead of security forces. An effective counter-terrorism strategy which combines political, military, legal, technological and economic dimensions, is still not in place. Considerable efforts will be required in improving these capabilities.

## Conclusion

It is a fact that terrorism has not succeeded in India even though it has caused great loss of life and property. India's biggest asset in dealing with terrorism has been its democracy and a greater political consensus for responsive governance, despite the loopholes in the system. The Indian experience shows that terrorism cannot be eliminated completely but it can be diminished through responsive governance and vigilance. The government of India sees global terrorism as a "grave challenge" to India's security.[19] Since terrorism is a global phenomenon, India needs to develop its diplomacy further to ensure that the external dimension of terrorism it faces is blunted. This will require a nuanced handling of its relations with Pakistan. India will have to ensure that Pakistan is deterred from using terrorism against India. At the same time, it will have to ensure that suitable strategies are adopted not to perpetrate a military conflict. Managing terrorism will require managing its relations with Pakistan. This will remain a key challenge for India.

> It is a self-evident truth that democratically multicultural societies are the prime targets of terrorism and are also the most vulnerable to its attacks. Terrorists exploit the civil liberties, religious tolerance and cultural diversity in our countries. They seek to destroy our democratic fabric by fomenting sectarian divisions and cultural tensions and ultimately deprive us of that very freedom which they have exploited.
>
> *—Brajesh Mishra, National Security Advisor, "Terrorism and Democratic Societies", Statement made at the Munich Security Conference, February 2, 2002*

## NOTES

1. Kanti Bajpai, *Roots of Terrorism*, Delhi: Penguin, 2002.
2. See Rajesh Rajagopalan, *Fighting Like a Guerrilla: The Indian Army and Counterinsurgency*, Routledge: Delhi, London, 2007, Sumit Ganguly, David P. Fidler, *India and Counterinsurgency: Lessons Learned*, Routledge: London, NY, 2009, Vandana Asthana, 'Cross-Border Terrorism in India: Counterterrorism Strategies and Challenges', ACDIS Occasional Paper series, June 2010. Available at: http://acdis.illinois.edu/publications/207/publication-cross-border-terrorism-in-india-counterterrorism-strategies-and-challenges.html (accessed October 29, 2010), S.D. Muni, *Responding to Terrorism in South Asia*, Manohar: Delhi, 2006,
3. Brahma Chellaney, "Fighting Terrorism in Southern Asia", *International Security*, Vol 26, No. 3, Winter 2001/2002, p. 96.
4. See for example, Sanjib Barua, *Durable Disorder—Understanding the Politics of Northeast India*, OUP: Delhi, 2005, *India Against Itself: Assam and the Politics of Nationality*, OUP: Delhi, 2000, Jaideep Saikia, ed., *Bangladesh: Treading the Taliban Trail*, Vision Books: New Delhi; Jaideep Saikia, ed., *Frontier in Flames: North East India in Turmoil*, Penguin: New Delhi, 2007.
5. This view is expressed by Chellany, n.3 and Ajai Sahni, "Responding to Terrorism in Punjab and Jammu and Kashmir, in S. D. Muni, ed. n.2, pp.31-75.
6. See for example Bajpai, n.2.
7. See for example, James A Piazza, "Economic development, Poorly Managed Political

Conflict and Terrorism in India", *Studies in Conflict and Terrorism*, Vol. 33, 2009, pp. 406-419.

8. B. Raman, "Countering Terrorism in India", September 3, 2009. available at www.southasiaanalysis.org/%5Cpapers34%5Cpaper3384.html, also see "International Jihadi Terrorism: An Indian Perspective", May 21, 2005, available at :http:// www.southasiaanalysis.org/%5Cpapers14%5Cpaper1388.html
9. This is a simplified version of the recommendation of the UN High Level Panel on Threats, Challenges and Change, which sought to define terrorism as "any action, in addition to actions already specified by the existing conventions on aspects of terrorism, the Geneva Conventions and Security Council resolution 1566 (2004), that is intended to cause death or serious bodily harm to civilians or non-combatants, when the purpose of such an act, by its nature or context, is to intimidate a population, or to compel a Government or an international organisation to do or to abstain from doing any act." See the full report on http://www.un.org/terrorism/highlevelpanel.shtml
10. Many analysts in India and Pakistan have written about Pakistani sponsorship of terror in Jammu and Kashmir. Some of them cited here are: Praveen Swamy, *An Informal War: India, Pakistan and the Secret Jihad in Jammu and Kashmir*, Routledge: London, 2007, Muhammad *Amir Rana, Jihad Kashmir wa Afghanistan: Jihadi Tanzimun aur Mazhabi Jamaton ka aik Jaeza*, Mashal Books: Lahore, 2002, Arif Jamal, *Shadow War: The Untold Story of Jihad in Kashmir*, Melville House: New York, 2009.
11. See Kalyan Chaudhari, "A Maoist revolutionary: Nagabhushana Patnaik, 1934-1998, *Frontline*, Chennai, Vol. 15, No. 22, October 24–November 6, 1998.
12. *Annual Report, 2009-2010*, Ministry of Home Affairs, Government of India, New Delhi, p.17.
13. Ibid.
14. See for the complete text: http://www.islam-watch.org/JihadiUmmah/Indian-Mujahideen.htm
15. See the well-argued article by S Kalyanaraman, "India and the Challenge of Terrorism in the Hinterland", *Strategic Analysis*, Vol. 34, Issue 5, September 2010, pp. 702-716. Also see, Praveen Swamy, 'India and its invisible jihad' in Satish Kumar (ed.), *India's National Security Annual Review 2008* Knowledge World Publishers: New Delhi, 2008.
16. S.D. Muni, ed., n. 2, p. 457.
17. KTS Tulsi, "Justice & Fairness in Terror Some Observations on TADA", *Faultlines*, Volume 1, 1999. Available at http://www.satp.org/satporgtp/publication/faultlines/ volume1/Fault1Tulsitext.htm
18. See, "Terrorism and Democratic Societies", a Statement made by Mr. Brajesh Mishra, Principal Secretary to the Prime Minister and National Security Advisor, Government of India, at the 38th Munich Conference on Security Policy, Munich, February 2, 2002. Available at: http://www.indianembassy.ru/docs-htm/en/en_05_04_t004_2002.htm
19. *Annual Report of the Ministry of Home Affairs (2009-10)*, Government of India, p. 5.

ANNEXURE I

**India: Terrorism-related National Legislations**

| Name of Act | Year of Enactment | Current Status | Remarks |
|---|---|---|---|
| National Investigation Act | 2008 | In operation | It shall be applicable to the whole of India, citizens of India, outside India, in service of the government, wherever they may be and for persons on ships and aircrafts registered in India. NIA officers shall have all the powers, privileges and liabilities which police officers have in connection with the investigation of any offence |
| Terrorist and Disruptive Activities (Prevention) Act TADA | 1985 | Defunct | Last amended in 1993; Allowed to lapse in 1995 |
| Terrorist Affected Areas (Special Courts) Amendment Act | 1984 | In operation | Originally enacted in 1984 |
| Prevention of Terrorism Act (POTA) | 2002 | Defunct | Originally enacted in 2002. It was meant to be applied in the States that wish to implement the law. Significantly, the Jammu and Kashmir government announced that it would not implement the law in the State. |
| Maharashtra Control of Organised Crime Act (MCOCA) | 1999 | In operation | |
| Andhra Pradesh Control of Organised Crime Act (APCOACA) | 2001 | In operation | |
| Arunachal Pradesh Control of Organised Crime Act (APCOCA) | 2002 | Defunct | The Act was repealed after the Gegong Apang-led Government took office in August 2003. |

| | | | |
|---|---|---|---|
| Disturbed Areas (Special Courts) Act | 1976 | In operation | It extends to the whole of India except the State of Jammu and Kashmir. |
| Armed Forces (Assam and Manipur) Special Powers Act | 1958 | In operation | Originally enacted in 1958. In operation as amended in 1972 |
| Armed Forces (Punjab and Chandigarh) Special Powers Act | 1983 | | |
| Chandigarh Disturbed Areas (Amendment) Act | 1989 | | Originally enacted in 1983 as Chandigarh Disturbed Areas Act |
| Punjab Disturbed Areas Act | 1983 | | |
| Armed Forces (Jammu and Kashmir) Special Powers Act | 1990 | In operation | |
| Assam Maintenance of Public Order Act | 1953 | | |
| Assam Preventive Detention Act | 1980 | | |
| Nagaland Security Regulation | 1962 | In operation | |
| Unlawful Activities (Prevention) Amendment) Act | 2008 | In operation | Originally enacted in 1967 |
| Anti-Hijacking (Amendment) Act | 1994 | In operation | Originally enacted in 1982 |
| Extradition (Amendment Act) | 1993 | In operation | Originally enacted in 1962 |
| National Security (Amendment) Act | 1988 | In operation | Originally enacted in 1980 |
| Prevention of Money Laundering Act | 2002 | In operation | The Act seeks to track the flow of funds to India to finance terrorism and narcotics through illegal money transfer channels including hawala. |

(*Contd.*)

| Name of Act | Year of Enactment | Current Status | Remarks |
|---|---|---|---|
| Prevention Detention (Continuance) Act | 1957 | In operation | Originally enacted in 1950 |
| Public Interest Disclosure (Protection of Informers) Act | 2002 | In operation | |
| SAARC Convention (Suppression of Terrorism) Act | 1993 | In operation | |
| Suppression of Unlawful Acts Against Safety of Civil Aviation (Amendment) Act | 1994 | In operation | Originally enacted in 1982 |
| Armed Forces (Assam & Manipur) Special Powers Act, 1958 | 1958 | In operation | Enable certain special powers to be conferred upon members of the armed forces in disturbed areas in the States of Assam and Manipur. |

This is a revised, but largely abridged, version of a Data Table from P.V. Ramana, "Data Chapter", in S.D. Muni, ed., *Responding to Terrorism in South Asia*, New Delhi: Regional Centre for Strategic Studies (Colombo) in association with Manohar Publishrers, 2005.

# 5

# *Countering Terrorism—The Maldivian Perspective*

*Mohamed Ziad*

## Introduction

Present-day terrorism is not an isolated phenomenon. It has to be viewed against the backdrop of fundamental and cultural antagonisms, domestic and international politics and national and international conflicts far beyond our own national boundaries. It is also associated with phenomena such as radicalisation and extremism, social discrimination, economic disparities, restrictions on rights and civil liberties and power politics.

The current international threat of terrorism is quite different from the terrorist threats that the states faced in the past. Contemporary terrorist groups claim religious justification for their action and have a wide-ranging religious and political agenda; they are no longer concerned with a single issue. Many seek mass civilian casualties and are prepared to adopt more unconventional means.

The Maldives might face an emerging threat from extremist ideologies—religious, political and social—who believe they can advance their aims by committing acts of terrorism in the Maldives. Some of the significant happenings like the improvised explosive device (IED) incident in Sultan Park and the incursion by a foreign vessel carrying arms and ammunition underscore this fact. In addition to this, the rise of violent organised crime, drugs, participation of youth in serious crimes could make the state the hotbed for terrorism.

## Purpose

The purpose of this paper is to suggest a comprehensive and holistic strategic framework for enhancing the security and reducing the vulnerability of small states like, the Maldives against terrorist attack, and in case they occur, to respond effectively and restore normalcy as soon as possible.

## Scope

The scope of the paper is limited to preventing, protecting, and countering acts of terrorism in a small state like Maldives.

## Strategic Importance of Maldives

Historically Maldives has been of strategic significance because of its location in the major sea lines of communication in the Indian Ocean which make it an important trans-shipment hub for the region. Maldives is the strategic naval link between West Asia and Southeast Asia. Maldives' nearest neighbours are Sri Lanka and India, both of which have had cultural and economic ties with Maldives for centuries. The country is renowned for its marine beauty and is a popular tourist destination. It is moving steadily from being in the least developed country category towards attaining the developing nation status.

The geo-strategic location of Maldives in the Indian Ocean is crucial to regional security. The presence of any external powers in Maldives would facilitate it in gaining supremacy of Indian Ocean which could pose a serious threat to the security and integrity of some of its neighbours as well as the region.

## Threat Analysis

### *Global Environment*

The events of 9/11 were an indicator of the scale and magnitude of the transformation that had taken place in the global geopolitical landscape. Terrorism was no longer bound within the confines of a single state; it has become 'internationalised' or 'globalised.' Thus; the concept of the global war on terror or GWOT is based on fighting global 'insurgency'. It further changed inter state relationships and changed the dynamics of *Realpolitiks.*

At the other end of the spectrum, the increasing frequency, lethality and the indiscriminating nature of the attacks conducted by the international network of terror has forced us to re-evaluate how we view and deal with terrorism; both domestic and international. Terrorists have shown themselves to be capable of infiltrating societies, raising finance, recruiting youth, planning operations in stealth and striking where least expected. This international menace is further compounded by the emergence of new nexuses linking: terrorism with piracy, drug trafficking, human trafficking, trade in blood diamonds and various other manifestations of organised crime.

### *Regional Environment*

The region has had a history of violence which manifested itself in conventional and unconventional conflicts. The SAARC countries have their own peculiar volatile conflicts and internal strife.

All the countries of the region have a few terrorist or separatist or irredentist groups. Amongst the SAARC countries, Afghanistan has the Al Qaeda and the Taliban. Pakistan has its Baluchi separatist movement and the Federally Administered Tribal Areas (FATA) insurgencies. India has separatist movements in Assam, Jammu and Kashmir, Manipur, Meghalaya, Nagaland, Punjab, Tripura, Mizoram and Arunachal Pradesh. Nepal has its Maoist fighters. Bhutan has United Liberation Front of Asom operating within its borders. Bangladesh has the Harkatul–Jihad–Al-Islami and a few other terrorist organisations. Sri Lanka has finally won the 30 year old civil war against the separatist Tamil movement LTTE.

The Southeast Asian region also has its share of terrorism and the Bali bombing of 2002 focussed world attention to this region. Malaysia has the Jamaah Islamiah (JI) and Lashkar Jihad, Indonesia has Aceh Separatists and the Front Pembela Islam, and Philippine has the Abu Sayyaf Group, the New People's Army and the Moro Islamic Liberation Front (MILF). These also include communist groups which resort to terrorist acts, and foster separatist movements.

### *Maldivian Environment*

The Maldives existed in isolation for centuries. Thus the community is ethnically, culturally and socially homogenous to a unique extent. The onset of globalisation and the advent of tourism in the Maldives turned us from an "unknown" to a "known" entity. The rapid exposure to outside world and the increase in the number of Maldivians travelling abroad for education, business and other purposes introduced foreign concepts, and new ways of thinking and behaviour to our shores.

## Possible Threats

The various threats that can manifest themselves as terrorist activities in Maldives need to be examined in their various dimensions. Given the existing global geopolitical environment in general and the regional scenario in particular especially in South and Southeast Asia, Maldives though not likely to be affected in the immediate future needs to take concrete measures to safe guard itself against terrorist activities and pre-empt any attack on its soil. Some of the likely threats are as follows:

### *Global / Regional Terrorist Groups*

(a) There are no indications at present to suggest any overt or covert presence of any pan-Islamic terrorist groups in Maldives. However, given the religious profile of the country, terrorist groups like Al Qaeda might decide to explore the possibilities of expanding their network to this region; and that cannot be ruled out.

(b) Terrorist groups operating in Southeast Asia like the Jamaah Islamiyah, the Abu Sayyaf Group and the Mindanao Liberation Front may want to expand their area of influence in the future in an effort to find safe havens. Though there is no immediate threat, their activities need to be studied and monitored for any such indications.

(c) A direct threat from regional and global terrorist groups is their possible incursion into the Maldivian territorial waters, either to find safe havens or for transit purposes. Constant surveillance and the presence of security forces in the vast territorial waters of Maldives is a challenge, given the dearth of resources. Under such circumstances, Maldives can very likely become a 'port of call' for terrorist organisations.

### *Extremist Ideologies*

(a) Maldives has always practiced the correct form of Islam and there has always been harmony in the country on this account. In recent years we are witnessing an increasing emphasis on the fundamentals of Islam. We have not seen any major signs of radicalism manifesting itself in the hardening of attitudes and leading towards extremism. But such a possibility cannot be ruled out. It has also been noticed that recently a few Maldivians have come to be associated with some Jihadist groups in Pakistan.

(b) The threat of extremism can sometimes be seen in both political and social sectors where the country is can be influenced by alien cultures due to the significant development and change that Maldives has experienced in recent times.

### *Piracy*

(a) The sea constitutes most of Maldives territory. Hence ensuring the security of its territorial waters is of prime concern to the Maldives within the limited available resources available. As the Maldives lie 1350 nautical miles away from Somalia, there is no direct incident of piracy in Maldives as of today. However there are many incidents of pirates being washed on to the shores of the Maldives in distress. So far 27 Somalis have thus landed in Maldives. Except for five all the others claim to be genuine fishermen washed on to the shores of Maldives under distress. However many of these people do not have any knowledge of fishing nor did they carry any fishing gear. Investigations have shown that most of these people are not genuine fishermen and neither do they have any knowledge of marine navigation. The mobile phones, watches and other belongings found on these vessels and people further support this conclusion.

(b) But the current expansion of piracy off the coast of Somalia and multiple incidents of piracy taking place almost 300 to 400 miles off the coast of Maldives show that Maldives will not continue to remain immune from this menace to maritime trade and commerce. Maldives as an archipelagic nation largely depends on tourism and fishing. Therefore the country needs to be proactive in fending off this nuisance and prevent such incidents from happening in Maldivian waters. An act of piracy in Maldivian waters could lead to terrorism and it would be devastating both in economic and political terms.

*Narco-Terrorism*

(a) The number of youth getting addicted to drugs is on the increase. Such youth are prone to being exploited, especially in view of the heroin-terrorism nexus that operates from Afghanistan.

(b) The entry and trafficking of drugs within the country will lead to an increase in criminal activities and mushrooming of criminal syndicates, who in turn will invariably develop a nexus with terrorist groups in days to come.

(c) The conduit for narco-trafficking can also be used for arms trafficking.

*Politically Motivated Acts of Terror*

(a) With the introduction of the multiparty system the political parties might be inclined to seek financial assistance from quarters with vested interests and thus increase the vulnerability of Maldives.

(b) Radical parties may also exploit religious sensitivities to polarise society.

(c) The political situation can be utilised by anti-national elements to propagate their aims and objectives. However, it must also be noted that political violence has reduced over the past few years and political parties have become more mature.

### *Adverse Impact of the Large Expatriate Work Force*

(a) Maldives has more than 98,000 expatriate workers working in numerous sectors, often under minimal supervision. They are also stationed in remote and sparsely populated islands all over the Maldives. A large segment of this expatriate work force is also residing in Maldives post the expiry of their visa and work permits, and hence, presents a very real security risk.

(b) The expatriate workforce is linked with several violent crimes, drug related incidents and other crimes. The possibility that they can also serve as conduits for smuggling of arms cannot be negated. The low level of surveillance and monitoring also makes it highly possible for trained terrorist operatives to seek refuge in Maldives and plan their operations. Maldives can also be used as a transit destination, where the terrorists are able to obtain safe havens.

## Counter-terrorism in the Maldives

Maldives being a small state, the threats it faces are different from those facing a larger state. Hence, the strategy to embark upon counter-terrorism has to be holistic and integrated. The counter terrorist efforts of the state and the concerned governmental and non-governmental agencies could be based on the following principles.

(a) National Integrated Approach
(b) Intelligence Based Operations
(c) Deterrence through Credible Show of Force
(d) Use of Minimum Force and Gradual Escalation
(e) Rule of Law and the need for Political Awareness
(f) Defeating Terrorism through International Partnerships

### *National Integrated Approach*

The Maldivian government recognises the need for an integrated and comprehensive approach to counter the threat of terrorism in the country. Close interagency coordination is vital for ensuring success in all phases of counter-terrorism operations. Terrorism is often a political problem, requiring a political solution, and the joint efforts of both the military and the civil government are vital to ensure that a lasting peace is brokered.

The National Security Council could oversee the overall implementation of the National Counter Terrorism Plans, and facilitate the synergy between all concerned agencies and departments. Other agencies have to ensure close coordination to accomplish the objectives and goals of national security.

### *Intelligence-based Operations*

One of the fundamental aspects of the Maldives national counter-terrorism strategy should be the primacy given to the role of intelligence in the conduct of counter terrorist operations. The cornerstone of a strong intelligence network is a vigilant general public who should be made aware and encouraged to identify and report any suspicious behaviour or incidents on the part of an individual or group.

Secondly, the government, through its integrative approach, should facilitate the creation of an Intelligence Fusion Centre, which coordinates the activities of all intelligence cells and branches of government agencies. This primary role of this centre would be to collect, analyse, facilitate action and disseminate information to the concerned authorities. Such an integrated intelligence network would enable the top echelon of the government to formulate proactive counter-terrorism plans.

### *Deterrence through Credible Show of Force*

The government of Maldives should be committed to protecting the lives and property of the people of Maldives from terrorist threats. The Maldives National Defence Force, acting in conjunction with the Maldives police and other concerned agencies would employ active force to pursue and defeat terrorism in the Maldives.

### *Use of Minimum Force and Gradual Escalation*

The government of Maldives should recognise the need for a humane approach while countering the threat of terrorism, in accordance with the human rights conventions, the law of armed conflict (LOAC) and the Geneva Convention. The force used in countering such threats should be the minimum required and the use of excessive force should not be allowed.

### *Rule of Law and the Need for Political Awareness*

The government of Maldives should establish the rule of law and ensure that all counter-terrorism measures are implemented on the bedrock of legislation. In addition, the government should establish close working partnerships with main political parties, religious groups, social interest groups and other main segments of civil society to formulate effective strategies and to increase the political awareness about terrorist threats in the country.

### *Defeat Terrorism through International Partnerships*

The government of Maldives should ally with the greater international community to fight against terrorism and be ready to participate in such international efforts. At the moment, Maldives is committed to the implementation of the United Nations Global Counter Terrorism Strategy, and, presently, Maldives is a signatory to almost all the major conventions on counter-terrorism.

## A Strategic Framework for Countering Terrorism

The national counter terrorism architecture of a small state like Maldives should be so formulated as to facilitate interagency cooperation and integration to achieve the national strategic aim. Thus, the strategic framework could be divided into five broad strands:

(a) Prevention,
(b) Protection,
(c) Prepare,
(d) Response, and
(e) Recovery.

***Prevention*** strand must be inclusive of the national effort aimed at detecting and deterring the threat of terrorism in the Maldives. This strand would involve: increasing the vigilance of the general public, setting up of a national intelligence agency and reducing the susceptibility of the Maldivian community to terrorist acts through:

(a) Promoting Maldivian values
(b) Tackling extremist ideologies
(c) Maintaining a stable political environment
(d) Neutralise those who promote violent extremism and destroy the places from where they operate
(e) Support individuals who are vulnerable to recruitment, or have already been recruited by extremists
(f) Address the grievances that are exploited by ideologues

***The Protection*** strand must aim at reducing vulnerability and providing protection against terrorist threats. Special emphasis would be placed on securing critical infrastructure and increasing the resilience of the Maldivian community to enable them to withstand terrorist threats. The protection strand may also encompass the following:

(a) Strengthening legislature
(b) Strengthening border security
(c) Protecting territorial waters/Ungoverned maritime space

(d) Enhancing physical security
(e) Safeguarding the economic infrastructure
(f) Enhance personal security

***The Prepare*** strand aims to mitigate the impact of a terrorist attack when it occurs. This includes managing an ongoing attack and planning for any future events. Many of the capabilities of the prepare strand, can also deal with the consequences of other threats or hazards. This strand may also include the following objectives;

(a) Plan for future threats like CBRN (chemical, biological, radiological or nuclear) weapons, cyber attacks
(b) Enhance coordination among different agencies
(c) Building resilience in emergency responders' telecommunications systems through updated technology

***The Response*** strand must include a national effort to increase the ability to respond effectively and immediately to terrorist attacks or threats of attack. This strand must also include the mechanics to coordinate the national counter terrorist efforts under the direction of the National Security Council and the MNDF. This strand must also include the following elements:

(a) Identifying and assessing risks
(b) Building capabilities
(c) Responding to terrorist attacks

***The Recovery*** strand involves a national effort to restore a state of normalcy and alleviate the sufferings of the people directly harmed by the terrorist incident. This strand should include a national recovery plan to be implemented by both governmental and nongovernmental agencies for supporting affected communities.

## Implementation of the Strategic Framework

Implementation of such a framework in a small state like the Maldives will require close cooperation between a multiple organisations, stakeholders and local authorities. Government departments, devolved administrations, the police, security and intelligence agencies, emergency services, armed forces and international partners and multilateral organisations will have to cooperate with each other. The key to successful implementation will depend on an effective interagency cooperation based on the horizontal and vertical communication between the agencies. This will also enhance the trust between different agencies.

## Conclusion

The best counter-terrorism option for a small state like Maldives is to establish better understanding and cooperation with the international community. All the agencies and forces involved in countering terrorism should closely work not only among themselves but also with friendly countries. A viable policy in countering terrorism is to defeat terrorism through international partnerships. Maldives must also be committed to the implementation of the United Nations Global Counter Terrorism Strategy.

An integrated and comprehensive approach should be the preferred tool for countering the threat of terrorism in the Maldives in the future. Terrorism often stems from political issues that require a political solution, and the joint efforts of both the military and the civil government are vital to ensure lasting peace.

# 6

# *The Impact of Terrorism on Sri Lanka: A Multifaceted Analysis*

*Shivaji Felix*

## Introduction

There is no consensus definition for terrorism. Many commentators have striven to define the term but have failed to come up with a definition that has universal validity. The predicament is that of a man who says, "I can recognise an elephant when I see one but I cannot define it".[1] This difficulty, in a way, echoes the famous words of St Augustine regarding the concept of time: "What then is time? If no one asks me I know: if I wish to explain it to one that asks I know not".[2] According to Bruce Hoffman the definition of terrorism, postulates a political motive, violence and an organisation having a distinct chain of command.[3] Carsten Bockstette goes on to include the 'violent victimisation and destruction of non-combatant targets (sometimes iconic symbols)'.[4]

Despite the absence of a definitive criteria, it is clear that the above mentioned characteristics have been apparent in Sri Lanka's civil conflict which lasted for nearly two score years.

In presenting the Sri Lankan perspective, it is important to understand the role of the historical context as a causative factor and its influence on terrorism. In 1948 newly independent Ceylon (as Sri Lanka was then known) was seen as a model state. There had been a peaceful transition of power and the country was stable and justifiably had reasonable expectations for a bright future.

However, in the words of Sumantra Bose, there was an agenda of 'ethnonational hegemony'[5] which was a by product of Sinhalese chauvinism in the post-colonial period. Slogans that Sri Lanka was for the 'Sinhala only' led to the marginalisation of the Tamil minority. This in turn led to a push for greater autonomy initially articulated politically by S.J.V. Chelvanayagam. On two separate occasions Chelvanayagam signed agreements with prime ministers S.W.R.D. Bandaranaike and Dudley Senanayake albeit such agreements were never implemented and were in fact actually aborted. The combination of chauvinism and the inability of Sinhalese leaders to stand up to the internal criticism by various nationalist factions of the so called 'Chelvanayagam Pacts' led to the sidelining of the Tamil minority. This frustration boiled over on two occasions culminating in the riots of 1977 and 1983. The 1983 riots, a direct result of the slaying of 13 soldiers by a small group led by Velupillai Prabhakaran (the then leader of the LTTE), fuelled the fires of the separatist movement and gave strength and motivation to the LTTE.

It is important to realise that the LTTE, as we know it, comprises three components.[6] As an armed group it has been vanquished, but the LTTE "network" and the "movement" still exists. The group has been dismantled through sheer military might supplemented by friendly intelligence received from the USA and India and military supplies procured from China and Pakistan.[7] However, it is now imperative to rely on diplomacy to engage the other two components of the LTTE and help them realise that Sri Lanka will benefit from their contribution in taking the country forward as a united nation.

## Political Impact

The impact, of the conflict with the LTTE, on the political framework of Sri Lanka has been significant. The losses caused have affected the Sinhalese and Tamils in equal measure. One of the key losses to the nation has been the elimination of Tamil moderates consequent to selective assassination. The LTTE's eagerness to be perceived as the sole representative of the Tamil people led them to systematically assassinate the finest Tamil intellectuals in the country.

This brazen attitude was clearly demonstrated when the LTTE assassinated Neelan Tiruchelvam—a lawyer, academic and constitutional expert—who had enormous credibility with the international community. As a moderate Tamil, he had long advocated a negotiated settlement for the ethnic problem in Sri Lanka through consensus building and constitutional reform.[8] However, his vision of a political settlement was at cross purposes with the LTTE's aim of statehood and he paid for his independent thinking with his life. Many other Tamil moderates like A Amirthalingam, Ketheeswaran Loganathan, Rajini Thiranagama were eliminated because they represented the moderate voice of the Tamils. The

LTTE believed that any Tamil who participated in a dialogue with the government or was prepared to consider anything short of a separate state as a political solution to the ethnic problem was a traitor to the cause and had to be eliminated.

Tamils, who openly opposed the LTTE were however directly on its hit list. Several unsuccessful assassination attempts were made on Douglas Devananda, an ex-militant and minister in the government. Similarly, the former foreign Minister, Lakshman Kadirigamar, who as a Tamil was despised for his lack of support for the LTTE's separatist agenda and his open opposition to it was a high profile target and remained on the LTTE hit list for many years until his eventual assassination. He often said that his opposition to the brutal methods adopted by the LTTE resulted in his being labelled a traitor. He famously said 'I am absolutely delighted to accept that appellation, I do it with pleasure'.[9] In fact it was through the tireless efforts of Lakshman Kadirigamar that the LTTE became a proscribed terrorist organisation in many parts of the world. Proscription in conjunction with the stringent domestic laws found in countries across the globe gave force to Resolution 1373 (2001) of the UN Security Council for putting a squeeze on the financing of terrorist acts. This led to a severely reduced the flow of funds to the LTTE.

Sri Lanka is currently in the midst of a diplomatic crisis vis-à-vis Western governments. Government leaders find it difficult to access Western leaders and state visits by such leaders to Sri Lanka are few and far between. It is in this context that the diplomatic skills of Lakshman Kadirigamar are being missed because of their effectiveness in the fight against terrorism.

In Sri Lanka, the United National Party (UNP) was elected in 1977 and remained in power until 1994 when the Sri Lanka Freedom Party (SLFP) led People's Alliance came into power. However, political assassinations have been a major cause of political instability in the country. President Ranasinghe Premadasa was assassinated by a LTTE suicide bomber in May 1993. One week prior to that, Lalith Atulathmudali, a prominent opposition politician and a critic of Premadasa, was assassinated by a lone gunman. Within eighteen months the ruling party (UNP) lost power in parliament, lost most of its frontline leadership and subsequently lost even the presidency. Furthermore, the UNP presidential candidate, Gamini Dissanayake, the then leader of the opposition, was assassinated in a suicide attack. Since 1994 the presidency has been with the Sri Lanka Freedom Party under Chandrika Kumaratunga and Mahinda Rajapakse (the latter being responsible for bringing about the downfall of the LTTE).

In 1999 the LTTE almost succeeded in assassinating the then president, Chandrika Kumaratunga on the eve of a presidential election. SLFP Minister,

C V Gooneratne and his wife were killed by a LTTE suicide bomber in 2000. A similar fate befell Jeyaraj Fernandopulle, a senior minister and Colombo Chetty politician. Scores of other SLFP leaders were also targeted leading to the adoption of extraordinary security measures in VIP movements.

Major General Lucky Algama, of the UNP, widely tipped to be the defence minister of a future UNP Government, and many others were assassinated in the run up to an election during this period. Major General Janaka Perera was assassinated over two years ago in the run up to a provincial council election. The LTTE therefore systematically eliminated the Singhalese political elite from the SLFP and the UNP thereby weakening the political leadership in the country.

In late 2001 the newly elected UNP-led government (albeit Chandrika Kumaratunge continued to remain President during this period) entered into a ceasefire agreement (CFA) with the LTTE brokered by Norway. The LTTE went through the motions of exploring the possibility of a political settlement to the ethnic problem in the form of a federal arrangement. However, like Oliver Twist they were always asking for more. They used the opportunity to beef up their arms supplies and, whilst talking peace, were preparing for war.[10] They then unilaterally withdrew from the peace process and returned to war. They felt that Wickremasinghe had led them into a peace trap and did not feel comfortable with the idea of his being elected president in view of the fact that he had built a formidable international network of Western contacts and an international safety net. Wickremasinghe, being a clever tactician, was a follower of Sun Tzu who states in his work, *The Art of War* that "the opportunity of defeating the enemy is provided by the enemy himself".[11] The LTTE felt that they were better off with Rajapakse having seriously misjudged Rajapakse's resolve, tenacity, native cunning and single minded pursuit and capacity to achieve a military victory.

The LTTE felt that Mahinda Rajapakse, whose power base was mainly Singhalese with a nationalist focus, was easy meat. It made a calculated decision to ruin Wickremasinghe's prospects of being elected as president because he was perceived to have a conciliatory approach and espoused a political solution, had international support, and would not resort to the all out onslaught against the LTTE as was the policy of SLFP led governments.

Mahinda Rajapakse was first elected president in 2005 following a very keenly contested election. The final margin of victory was as little as 1.86 per cent.[12] The voter turnout in the Northern Province (the northern most area of Sri Lanka), which was more supportive of the thinking of the UNP led by Ranil Wickremasinghe, was 1.21 per cent.[13] This was a direct result of the LTTE preventing the majority of the population from going to the polls. The final margin of victory in the presidential election was 180,786 with the LTTE preventing more than 400,000 people from voting in the Northern Province.[14] The LTTE in effect chose the president of Sri Lanka, which in retrospect led to their downfall. If they had not prevented the people of Jaffna peninsula from voting Velupillai Prabhakaran would probably have been alive today.

The other mistake that the LTTE made was to adopt an all or nothing approach for negotiations. They did not believe in an incremental approach whereby they took the maximum that could possibly be offered, consolidated themselves, and then asked for more. The all or nothing approach resulted in the Tamil people getting next to nothing in terms of the devolution of political power after the military defeat of the LTTE. It is necessary to remember that several successive governments in Sri Lanka had even gone to the extent of offering various forms of federalism as a political solution to the ethnic problem. These offers were rejected by the LTTE on the grounds that they did not go far enough. When a nascent form of federalism was offered, the LTTE insisted on a confederation and rejected the offer; with the result that, after the military defeat the LTTE, are now discussing how the Thirteenth Amendment to the Constitution, which became law as far back as in 1987, could be fully implemented. What was gained on the swings has been lost on the roundabouts!

## Economic Impact

The economy of Sri Lanka, as is the case with most civil war afflicted nations, has been decimated by terrorism and the war efforts. With a population of approximately 20 million, the Sri Lankan market has not been able to attract the same level of foreign investment as its counterparts in South Asia which provide access to larger untapped markets.

In the late 1960s, as Singapore was embarking on its remarkable economic expansion programme Sri Lanka was perceived as a benchmark by the newly elected Lee Kuan Yew. Whilst Singapore's rapid economic development has been a phenomenon, it is still important to realise that both nations initially had comparable GDP per capita incomes. Unfortunately due to the lack of foreign investment coupled with escalating defence expenditure, the GDP per capita of Sri Lanka stagnated. This cannot be attributed to the civil conflict alone. It is also a result of ill considered policy decisions in a variety of fields, especially language policy. However, it is beyond doubt that the conflict has been the dominant factor that has held the nation back during the last three decades.[15] In 2009 the GDP per capita of Sri Lanka was $4,770 compared to $50,500 in Singapore.[16] Whilst this figure, along with the annual GDP growth rates, is impressive for a nation afflicted by such a severe conflict, it is a widely held opinion that this is well short of Sri Lanka's full potential. When considering this point one has to remember that Sri Lanka has a well educated population with a literacy rate of over 92 per cent.[17]

Another area seriously affected by terrorism was the tourism industry—one of Sri Lanka's primary sources of foreign exchange. With the escalation of the conflict in the country, the number of tourists visiting the country declined dramatically. This was made worse by the LTTE attack on the sole international airport in the country in 2001. This resulted in the destruction of a large part of the fleet of Sri Lankan Airlines—the national carrier of Sri Lanka. Whilst there were no tourist casualties, it resulted in focussing international media attention on the civil conflict and, as a result, tourist arrivals fell further. There was a discernible increase in the number of foreign tourists visiting Sri Lanka during the when the CFA brought about by the UNP government led by Prime Minister Ranil Wickremasinghe, held in 2002. The numbers however steadily declined after 2005 with the escalation of war.[18]

In the light of terrorist atrocities such as the attack on the international airport, the central bank and other economic targets, Sri Lanka faced an increase in war risk insurance premiums.[19] This has been clearly seen in the fields of aviation and shipping insurance. This eroded the profitability of the tourism industry as well as increasing the cost of trade for businesses due to increased import and export charges being passed on to importers and finally the local consumer in the case of imports and squeezing profit margins in the case of exporters.

Sri Lanka has however been able to seize opportunities in adversity. This is best seen in the aviation industry. When the Sri Lankan Airlines initially entered into leasing agreements for its Airbus fleet, the necessity to obtain aircraft without delay trumped the economic terms on which the leases were granted. These leases were clearly uneconomic but alterations to the agreements were not possible without serious economic loss. However, the attack on the airport in 2001 led to the destruction of a part of the fleet. This frustrated the commercial leasing contracts which were otherwise legally enforceable and unalterable. It was after the termination of these uneconomic contracts that Sri Lankan airlines was eventually able to enter into fresh leases, on better terms, which led to the company turning around and bolstering its financial position to become a leaner, fitter and better managed organisation.

In spite of all the adverse publicity, the economy has been growing over the last 20 years. GDP growth annually has consistently exceeded 6 per cent since 2000.[20] An area of concern is the burgeoning trade deficit, with exports unable to keep pace with the rising demand for imports.[21] It is with this in mind that Sri Lanka has recently welcomed companies like Mahindra who are looking to invest in Sri Lanka and in turn helping to increase its productive capacity.

The culmination of the war also led to a boom in construction. There has been a concerted effort by the current government to divert resources towards improving the infrastructure of the island. There has been a particular focus on developing the east coast—long sidelined due to a strong LTTE presence. The development of the road network and the international ports, both air and sea, represent the first semblance of a peace dividend. With assistance from India our country is now seeking to restore and upgrade its railway network.[22] The post war era has also led to a boom in the Colombo Stock Exchange, Asia's best performing stock exchange in 2009,[23] where prices have literally gone through the roof.

During the period of conflict, two industries showed particular resilience. The first being the tea industry—this is the industry in which Sri Lanka can claim to be a global player. The second is the garment industry. The European Union (EU), Sri Lanka's largest trading partner, gave extra trade concessions, which varied from fisheries to garments to enable Sri Lankan exports to penetrate the European single market. These additional concessions have been withdrawn from August 2010 due to disagreements between the EU and the government[24] on certain key human rights benchmarks. The withdrawal of such concessions has been viewed as a reprimand of the Sri Lankan government for prosecuting the war on terror whilst not holding itself accountable to the international community at large for perceived human rights violations. Regardless of the apparent hypocrisy of the West, it would appear that such an interference in Sri Lanka's affairs was exactly the sort of intervention in relation to another country's sovereignty that IK Gujral, the then Indian external affairs minister, was hoping to avoid and alluded to in his address delivered at the Royal Institute of Foreign Affairs in 1996.[25] On that occasion he laid out five key principles of India's approach to regional politics. The most significant principle being the non-interference in the internal affairs of any other South Asian country. This sentiment was echoed by his successor Yashwant Sinha, thereby showing true bipartisan solidarity.

Looking past the crippling economic effects of the war, there have been some social benefits that have been a corollary of our conflict. The Tamil community in Sri Lanka had a very well entrenched and archaic caste system. The rise of the LTTE, which were mainly led by people of a lower caste, resulted in a weakening of the caste system in the Tamil community. In post-war Sri Lanka, we are perhaps beginning to see the re-emergence of caste divisions especially in the politics of the Jaffna peninsula.

Furthermore, it can be seen that the urgent task of reconciliation has been reduced to an attempt to economically develop the Northern and Eastern

Provinces. The question of accountability for gross violations of human rights in the last phase of the war has become a non-issue. The recently appointed Lessons Learned and Reconciliation Commission has a flawed mandate[26] and is merely an optical illusion for the purpose of deflecting international pressure in a context where human rights in an era of terrorism is fast becoming a fashionable subject.[27]

## Current Issues Facing the Country

The end of the military domination of the LTTE has not rid Sri Lanka of all its problems relating to the conflict. In prosecuting the final phase of the war there was a clear curtailment of the freedom of the press. There was a widely held belief that such restrictions, regardless of how unpalatable they appeared, were in the interests of the greater good of society. This was silently accepted given the underlying belief that the *status quo ante* would be restored once the war had come to an end. There has however been a drastic clampdown on any dissent and the press is still not able to write freely on any matter that they see fit. This hard stance became abundantly clear with the assassination of Lasantha Wickramatunga, a prominent newspaper editor, who frequently ran anti-government headlines in his Sunday newspaper. This was seen as the culmination of a very public crackdown on journalists. The number of stories of journalists disappearing or being assaulted has soared. Many journalists have fled the country or are underground due to this perceived threat. This has led to Sri Lanka now being ranked as the fourth most dangerous country for a journalist.[28]

There has also been an ever increasing demand by the international community, especially the Western nations, to push for an independent panel to investigate into alleged human rights abuses during the final countdown of the war with the LTTE. This demand has been flatly turned down by the government of Sri Lanka which has sought to keep all external parties out of what it considers to be an infringement of its own sovereignty. Whilst this stance does have merit, the government has been ill advised as to how it should articulate its disagreement. The barricading of the UN compound in Colombo in July 2010 by a senior government minister was an inappropriate method of approaching what is essentially a matter best served through diplomatic channels.

In an attempt to address such issues the Sri Lankan government set up the Lessons Learnt and Reconciliation Commission (LLRC), in an attempt to form a committee purportedly modelled on Desmond Tutu's Truth and Reconciliation Commission of South Africa. However, this has been rejected by the international community and by Desmond Tutu himself,[29] on the basis that the Commission has not been properly constituted and is thereby unsuited for a sufficiently impartial hearing. Needless to say, we will be able to discern its credibility and usefulness when the final report of the LLRC comes out.

A particularly saddening result of Sri Lanka's experience of terrorism has been the degree of normalcy, insensitivity and complacency associated with death and destruction. Given that over 70 per cent of the country is Buddhist the instinctive reaction is to draw an analogy with peace and tranquillity. Unfortunately, the past quarter century of conflict has led to a general sense of desensitisation amongst the public. As mentioned earlier, the slaying of 13 soldiers led to ethnic riots in 1983. Decades later a far greater loss of life barely created any stir amongst the population at large. It is my view that this attitudinal change will take generations to address and reform.

## Concluding Observations

The subject of the war on terrorism and its aftermath still holds many challenges for Sri Lanka. Given the acceptance by all parties that the LTTE is no longer a force on the ground in Sri Lanka there is a legitimate need to try and reform those who are still sympathetic towards their previously held ideal of an independent state. Due to the absence of a ground force, fund raisers abroad can argue that monies are being collected merely for political lobbying as opposed to terrorist funding.[30] It is therefore of paramount importance to quell any underlying animosity by directly engaging the Tamil minority and providing a political settlement, irrespective of any previous military victory. In this regard it is imperative to differentiate between the oppressed minority Tamil citizens of Sri Lanka and the small sub-sect who actually comprised the LTTE. Through the demise of the latter the former has an opportunity to uplift itself.

I would like to conclude by referring to a statement attributed to Rajan, a former LTTE head in Malaysia. He stated that his father had fought for Tamil rights politically, he himself fought militarily and he believes his son will fight peacefully. In this regard, there is a comparison that can be laid out across the South Asian region. When political tensions boil over to military action there can be no sustainable solace through a military outcome. There can only be laid a fertile foundation for the purpose of arriving at an eventual reconciliation with peace, dignity, honour and amicability for the enduring good of all Sri Lanka's people.

### Notes

1. H L A Hart, *The Concept of Law* (1961), OUP, 13.
2. St. Augustine, *Confessiones,* xiv. 17.
3. Bruce Hoffman, *Inside Terrorism* (2006), Columbia University Press, 2nd edn. 41.

4. Carsten Bockstette, *"Jihadist Terrorist Use of Strategic Communication Management Techniques*, George C. Marshall Centre Occasional Paper Series (2008), 20.
5. Sumantra Bose, *Contested Lands: Israel—Palestine, Kashmir, Bosnia, Cyprus, and Sri Lanka* (2007) Harvard University Press, 29.
6. Rohan Gunaratna (2010), "A Post War Challenge for Sri Lanka : Dismantling the LTTE overseas and rebuilding a Sri Lankan identity" *Asian Tribune*, Vol. 11, No. 90, 5 August 2010.
7. See, e.g., Interview with Colonel R. Hariharan - http://www.sundayobserver.lk/2010/08/15/sec03.asp.
8. Amnesty International condemns killing of Neelan Tiruchelvam MP – 29/7/99 http://www.amnesty.org/en/library/asset/ASA37/019/1999/en/1dcf81ce-e0df-11dd-aaeb-414a3b04625c/asa370191999en.html.
9. Hard Talk, *BBC News*, http://news.bbc.co.uk/2/hi/programmes/hardtalk/4373059.stm.
10. For differing views on the peace process and its efficacy see, e.g., Gunasekara, S L, *Abomination: About the demand for an ISGA* (2004); Centre for Just Peace and Democracy, *Envisioning New Trajectories for Peace in Sri Lanka* (2006); Rainford, Charan and Satkunanathan, Ambika, *Mistaking Politics for Governance : The Politics of Interim Arrangements in Sri Lanka 2002–05* (2009).
11. Sun Tzu, '*The Art of War*' – circa 500 B.C.
12. Department of Elections Website – Sri Lanka http://www.slelections.gov.lk/pdf/2005%Presidential-Summary.pdf.
13. *Sunday Leader*, 'Tigers shut down north' – 20/11/05 http://www.thesundayleader.lk/archive/20051120/spotlight.htm.
14. *Asian Tribune*, 'Strategic miscalculation by the LTTE' – 2/6/09 – http://www.asiantribune.com/?q=node/15489.
15. Rohan Gunaratna (2010), "A Post War Challenge for Sri Lanka : Dismantling the LTTE overseas and rebuilding a Sri Lankan identity," *Asian Tribune*, Vol. 11, No. 90, 5 August 2010.
16. IMF, World Economic Outlook Database – http://www.imf.org/external/pubs/ft/weo/2010/01/weodata/index.aspx.
17. UNICEF, Country Statistics – http://www.unicef.org/infobycountry/sri_lanka_statistics.html
18. Sri Lanka Tourism, Tourist No's 2001: 336,800 2004: 566,200 2009: 447,890.
19. *BBC News*, 'Airlines suspend Sri Lanka flights' 18 September 2001. http://news.bbc.co.uk/2/hi/south_asia/1550338.stm.
20. Key Economic Indicators (2008), Central Bank of Sri Lanka.
21. Reuters, 'Sri Lanka May trade deficit widens to $430.9mln' – http://www.xe.com/news/2010-08-03%2008:26:00.0/1312321.htm?c=1&t=108.
22. *Asian Tribune*, 'India to assist Sri Lanka in the construction of the Northern Railway Lines' – http://www.asiantribune.com/news/2010/08/18/india-assist-sri-lanka-construction-northern-railway-lines.
23. Bloomberg, 'Sri Lanka stocks, Asia's best performers, to extend gains' – 30/12/09 - http://www.bloomberg.com/apps/news?pid=newsarchive&sid=aIEBMrIYVicc.
24. *BBC News*, 'EU to withdraw Sri Lanka trade concessions deal', 5 July 2010.
25. I.K. Gujral (1996), Royal Institute of International Affairs, London, "Foreign policy objectives of India's united front government".
26. See, e.g., Collective for Economic, Social and Cultural Rights in Sri Lanka, Civil Society Report regarding the implementation of the International Covenant on economic, social and cultural rights (10 September 2010).

27. See, e.g., Arden, The Rt Hon Dame Mary, "Human Rights in the Age of Terrorism" *(2005) 121 LQR 604*; Lord Hope of Craighead, "Torture" *(2004) 53 ICLQ 807.*
28. "Committee to protect Journalists – Impunity Index 2010" – http://www.cpj.org/reports/2010/04/cpj-2010-impunity-index-getting-away-with-murder.php.
29. Desmond Tutu and Lakhdar Brahimi, "Sri Lanka one year on from war" – http://www.guardian.co.uk/commentisfree/2010/may/18/sri-lanka-lasting-peace.
30. Rohan Gunaratna (2010), "A Post War Challenge for Sri Lanka : Dismantling the LTTE overseas and rebuilding a Sri Lankan identity," *Asian Tribune*, Vol. 11, No. 90, 5 August 2010.

# 7

# *Bhutan's Approach to Combating Terrorism*

*Karma Tsering Namgyal*

Bhutan is a very small country with a population of only 600,000 which has been led by a line of dynamic Kings. Modernisation began in mid-1960s during the reign of the third King, Jigme Dorji Wangchuk who is referred to as the father of modern Bhutan. Since then Bhutan has adopted a very cautious approach and has strictly followed the policy of sustainable development. The fourth King of Bhutan introduced the concept of Gross National Happiness as the guiding philosophy for country's development process. The GNH philosophy is guided mainly by four main pillars; they are:

1. The promotion of sustainable development;
2. Preservation and promotion of cultural values;
3. Conservation of the natural environment; and
4. Establishment of good governance.

Security is a top priority for Bhutan and without it Bhutan cannot achieve its aim of Gross National Happiness. Therefore, Bhutan's governance policy is based on providing security and safety to its people. Under the leadership and wisdom of the kings, the people of Bhutan have been enjoying continued peace and prosperity.

Working towards achieving the goal of a happy world and particularly South Asia is I believe, the very essence of this workshop, particularly when one considers that a durable happiness can only thrive in a secure and peaceful environment.

While the cultures and civilisations of South Asia are regarded as being among the most ancient, our region is becoming better known today for its mosaic of crises, fuelled by acts of terrorism and extremism. Terrorism, extremism, and their varied manifestations are phenomena that transcend national boundaries. We have observed the crippling effects these criminal acts can have on states, throwing back by decades of hard earned gains of socio economic development, the heart wrenching loss of life, destruction of property, coupled with the violation of some of the most basic human rights and the victimisation of innocents. Such violence makes the stability of the region fragile.

The RGoB reiterates its firm resolves to root out terrorism, in all its forms and manifestations. The RGoB also recognises the linkages between terrorism, illegal trafficking in drugs and psychotropic substances, illegal trafficking of persons and firearms, and reaffirms its commitment to address these challenges in a comprehensive manner. The convening of this important workshop to share experiences and ideas is therefore a timely and an important demonstration of our collective will to strengthen cooperation and the capacity to fight terrorism and transnational organised crimes in a coordinated manner.

Many of the South Asian states have, and some continue to be afflicted by the worst terrorist attacks of our times. Allow me to express our deep sympathies for the tremendous loss and destruction suffered, particularly by the victims of families affected by such acts. On behalf of my government and people, I extend Bhutan's solidarity with the governments and people that have had to bravely face such deplorable incidents.

As expressed by our hon'ble prime minister, Lyonchhen Jigme Y. Thinley at the inaugural session of the XVIth SAARC summit in Thimpu, Bhutan believes that:

> No cause can be enhanced or served through acts of terror nor is it in any degree deserving of sympathy and support. Any act of violence that maims and kills innocent civilians desecrates and defiles even the noblest of causes. Those who are responsible for the perpetration of such heinous crimes against humanity must know that they will be brought to justice...

I would here assure that the royal government of Bhutan and its people will continue to support and combat terrorism in the same spirit.

As non-traditional security threats continue to grow in complexity, the primacy of sharing experiences, understanding and learning counter-terrorism measures from each other for an effective response becomes more imperative.

In keeping with the royal government's policy not to allow any terrorist activities against other states to be launched or planned from our soil, the Royal

Bhutan army conducted a military operation to flush out insurgent groups from Bhutanese territory in December 2003. Since then, Bhutan has not faced any large scale terrorist attacks or activity in the country. However, since then, there have been a number of incidents of bomb detonations involving militants based in second countries. These incidents have however largely been demonstrative of tactics, with minimal casualties to either security forces or civilians. They appear to have been designed to instil fear and insecurity among the public. Since 2003, Bhutan has no terrorist organisations operating from within the country and there have been no intrusions of terrorist organisations into the country, aside from the few militants from second countries referred to. While Bhutan is privileged in enjoying peace, I wish to emphasise that we are by no means complacent, and recognise our existing vulnerabilities, largely arising from resource and infrastructure constraints.

The royal government has taken a number of practical and legislative steps to implement the provisions of the Convention and the Additional Protocol since their ratification by Bhutan. At the international level, Bhutan is signatory to eight UN treaties on terrorism, and we continue to cooperate with UN mechanisms responsible for counter-terrorism efforts. Bhutan remains committed to the full implementation of the provisions of these important instruments, with due regard to its obligations under international law, particularly international human rights and humanitarian law. These provide Bhutan with the legislative framework on which to base our efforts to combat terrorism. However, as a small landlocked country, we are mindful that we continue to face capacity and resource constraints, which can negatively affect operationalisation of some initiatives.

With regard to combating Terrorism, in pursuance of our obligations under the UN Convention and SAARC Convention of Terrorism and the Protocol, Bhutan enacted the enabling legislation in 1991. The RGOB's legislative framework is in compliance with most provisions of our international treaty obligations. These are in sync with the provisions of the aforementioned Conventions and its additional Protocols. Given the open and porous border, Bhutan and India have been meeting regularly under the established home secretaries forum and as well as continuing the border districts coordination with primary focus on border management and security along the Bhutan-India border. Through these mechanisms, both sides have effectively reduced criminal activities and maintained peace along our shared border.

Bhutan, on its part, remains committed to working closely to translate our commitments into tangible results in order to promote conditions of peace and security for the benefit, and eventual happiness of all our people. This was in brief the state of our country's initiatives taken for combating terrorism.

# 8

# *Cycles of Violence: Conflict in 'Post-Conflict' Nepal*

*Deepak Thapa*

The restoration of democracy following Jana Andolan II, or People's Movement II, in April 2006 came with the promise of a new Nepal. Since there was no blueprint of what that meant and was only an idea that had quickly picked up steam in the fight against the monarchy, everyone interpreted 'new Nepal' in their own way. It was indeed meant to mean everything for everyone as it was to end all the ills that afflicted the state of Nepal and herald a peaceful and prosperous future. What mattered even more was that since the Communist Party of Nepal (Maoist)—CPN (M)—was party to the successful people's revolt, the 'people's war' was going to come to an end soon.

On April 28, Girija Prasad Koirala of the Nepali Congress, the prime minister-designate from the seven-party alliance (SPA), proposed to the newly restored parliament that 'this meeting of the house of representatives vows and decides to hold constituent assembly elections to draft a new constitution'. Koirala's proposal was welcomed by all and that opened the way for the Maoists to join the political mainstream since the election to a constituent assembly had been one of their major demands.

Shortly thereafter, the parliament also declared itself sovereign and made a number of declarations that struck at the core of the Hindu monarchical system, including the removal of the 'royal' from all government institutions, while the state itself was declared to be secular, thus ending the traditional link between the state and the monarchy. Some tension followed these momentous changes as the Maoists who believed that they who had raised all these issues should be party to such announcements. But in the spirit of the peace process, such hurdles were easily overcome.

Negotiations between the SPA and the Maoists moved rapidly forward and on November 21, 2006, the two sides signed the Comprehensive Peace Accord (CPA). Negotiations between the two sides continued thereafter and soon there was also an understanding on the Agreement on Monitoring the Management of Arms and Armies (AMMAA), which became the basis for the Interim Constitution and for putting Maoist fighters and their arms in designated camps, which lead to the setting up of a constituent assembly in June 2007 and a new constitution.

The CPA signalled the formal end of the Maoist insurgency, and with the AMMAA and the interim constitution the country's resolute march towards a new Nepal and lasting peace seemed certain. Within days this certainty had all unravelled and the violence that Nepalis believed they had left behind took a turn that had been completely unforeseen. This paper attempts to trace some of the trends that have emerged from this new cycle of violence in Nepal, the causes behind it, and the current situation.

## Tarai on Fire

Soon after the draft of the interim constitution was made public in December 2006, the Madhesis from the southern Tarai plains made their discontent known. During the negotiations leading up to the framing and promulgation of the interim constitution, the Madhesi groups had been trying to impress their concerns upon the SPO-Maoist. But the focus of the latter was more on finding ways to bring the Maoists into the political mainstream and the protestations by Madhesi groups, that also included a party that was part of the SPA, were not taken seriously.

Federalism was a key issue for Madhesis.[1] As the draft of the interim constitution did not even mention it and neither did it look into the issue of increasing the number of electoral constituencies in the Tarai despite the significant migration from the hills to the plains over the years, protests erupted in Nepalgunj in western Nepal. As part of the SPA, the party leading the Nepalgunj protests, the Nepal Sadhbavana Party (Ananda Devi), was technically a part of the interim constitution drafting process. The leading parties in the SPA, the CPN (UML) and the two factions of the Nepali Congress, and the CPN (Maoist), however, made no attempt to address the issues. Thus, the day after the interim constitution was adopted on January 15, 2007, copies of the document were burnt by some leading Madhesi activists in Kathmandu in protest. Their arrest and the subsequent protests that erupted in parts of the Tarai caught the government, and the Maoists, quite unawares. The government attempted taking a hard line against the protests and that only added further fuel to the fire. It took 19 days of protests and rioting during what has been called the Madhes movement, which led to a complete shutdown in this vital region of Nepal, before the government reached out to Madhesi groups to seek a political resolution to the issues. But it took one more round of agitation by Madhesis before the government responded by fulfilling their two major demands: redrawing of electoral districts and including federalism in the interim constitution. The Madhes Movement was concentrated mainly in the 10 districts of central and eastern Tarai.[2] These 10 districts are home to nearly 25 per cent of the population of Nepal, and almost three quarters of them are Madhesis. It is this numerical clout that became evident during the agitation.

But long before the Madhesis had come out on the streets demanding their rights, there were already two groups waging an armed struggle against the state. These were the two factions of the Janatantrik Tarai Mukti Morcha (JTMM), one headed by Jay Krishna Goit and the other by Jwala Singh. Goit had split from the Madhesi National Liberation Front (MNLF)—one of the numerous fronts set up by the Maoists for the liberation of the various 'nationalities' of Nepal—in protest against discrimination against Madhesis by the Pahadis within the Maoist organisation. He articulated the view that the Tarai plains had been colonised by the Pahadi-dominated Nepali state and believed an independent Tarai was the solution. The JTMM, however, split in August 2006, with Nagendra Paswan, aka Jwala Singh, forming the JTMM (JS). While they made charges and counter-charges against each other for the split, it is believed that one of the reasons was the caste difference between Goit (a Yadav) and Paswan (a Dalit). In terms of ideology, there is not much difference between the two since both believe violence to be a legitimate strategy and also that the state of Nepal has no right over the Tarai.

The Maoists had not taken kindly to Goit's departure and in July 2006, Matrika Yadav, Goit's successor in the MNLF declared war on the JTMM. The antagonism between the MNLF and the JTMM, over the same turf—Madhesi sympathies—is believed to be a major reason for the rising in violence in the Tarai. While the Maoist movement, with its call for Madhesi liberation helped radicalise the Madhesis—as it did the other marginalised groups of Nepal—its failure fulfil the major aspirations of Madhesis led to an erosion in its support base among Madhesis. But the Maoists had also effectively demonstrated the power of armed action, and it was this that both the JTMMs were able to utilise to build their own support base. And, in order to prove themselves different from the Maoists MNLF, they took the extreme step of targeting people of hill origin living in the Tarai.

The Madhes Movement had put the government on a back foot by virtue of its sheer scale and intensity. After the initial efforts to suppress it—that provoked a stronger reaction—it stepped back and let the protests continue without much interference even as they sought to find a suitable way to placate the Madhesis. By doing so, however, they left the field wide open for a number of other armed groups to operate. These are all modelled after JTMM in that all claim to be fighting for Madhesis, but they are increasingly seen as more criminal than political, seeking to take advantage of the weak law and order situation and the anti-Pahadi sentiment in the Tarai. There is no record of how many such groups exist since it is not even clear if many of them are in any way organised. Their only claim to legitimacy seems to be their names such as: Madhesi Mukti Tigers, Madhesi Virus Killers, Tarai Cobra, and even Liberation Tigers of Tarai Eelam. But these armed groups are increasingly responsible for perpetuating a sense of insecurity in the Tarai with abductions, extortion, and murders becoming quite common.

## Eastern Nepal

If there is any other area apart from the Tarai that has shown the potential to challenge the Nepali state, it is the eastern hill region of Nepal, historically the land of the Limbus. Both regions have a history different from the rest of Nepal and emphasise the idea of colonisation by the hill people (for the Tarai) and by Kathmandu (for eastern Nepal). As with the Tarai and its heavy concentration of Madhesis, the proportion of Limbus in the eastern hills is also considerable. Nearly 70 per cent of the Limbus still live in the region that is increasingly being called Limbuwan although because of in-migration by various other groups, they are now constitute a little over a quarter of the regional population.

The major players in eastern Nepal are the Maoist ethnic liberation fronts, non-violent movements for regional autonomy and assorted armed groups who have learnt the art of extortion both from the Maoists and the Tarai armed groups that came later. As with the Tarai, no one is sure about the number of groups that actually operate in eastern Nepal. Given the sporadic appearance and disappearance of such groups, observers point to the futility of keeping track and even police officials express their inability to do so. There are some political players as well that have been organised along ethnic lines with the major ones being the three factions of the Federal Limbuwan State Council. At least one of these factions has established a force called Limbuwan volunteers. Extortion is rife, and implicit is the idea of a struggle against the 'colonisers', mainly the dominant Bahuns and Chhettris, although thus far targeted killings have not take place as has been the case in the Tarai against Pahadis. As during the Maoist conflict, fear of reprisals prevent the reporting of these activities to the state.

One significant factor in the past couple of years has been the entry of international instruments into local politics. The Nepali state has recognised 59 of the over 100 social groups in the country as indigenous peoples. In 2007, Nepal became one of the few of countries to adopt the ILO Convention 169 on Indigenous and Tribal Peoples. The ratification enjoins the Nepali government to formulate a national plan on how it would fulfil the convention's provisions. But while that has yet to be done, the ILO 169 has been taken by indigenous groups to mean a return of their rights over the territory they consider their homeland, especially with regard to control over natural resources. The ILO 169 requires the government to consult the indigenous population over the use of natural resources without granting the latter any exclusive right over the resources. In Nepal, however, the interpretation of the convention has been to mean the sole right of the indigenous groups over natural resources. That is forming the basis on which some of these groups in the eastern hills have been mobilising.

## Storm Troopers

A major source of public insecurity has been the youth wing of the CPN (Maoist), the Young Communist League (YCL). Released from cold storage following the sending to cantonment of the Maoist People's Liberation Army (PLA) in December 2006, the YCL was meant to mobilise the youth on behalf of the Maoists as it sought to mainstream its activities. A recruitment drive rapidly bloated the ranks of the YCL, which already included some PLA members and the Maoist militia, and the organisation soon gained notoriety and the members served as the storm troopers of the Maoists in all the manner of activities, including intimidation, procurement of contracts, etc.

In a review of YCL activities undertaken in the first few months of its reconstitution, the United Nations Office of the High Commissioner for Human Rights in Nepal concluded that while the YCL has been undertaking community activities which are generally viewed as positive and demonstrations involving the YCL have not always been violent, it is the YCL's challenging of certain political and other organisations through threats and violence, as well as the abuses committed in the context of "law enforcement" that have principally been cause for concern. Though the types and levels of abuses vary from district to district, those documented by OHCHR include abuses related to the right to freedom of opinion, assembly and association as well as the rights to personal liberty, security and physical integrity.[3]

The success of the Maoists in the CA elections was also attributed in part to the YCL and its alleged use of violence or threats if it thereof. In June 2008, the CPN (UML) also floated its own organisation, the Youth Force, to counter the activities of the YCL. Unlike in the case of other groups, both the YCL and the YF[4] are backed by major political parties, and, so the administration has been unable to curb their activities. The irony of it all was that the YCL and the YF were most active, and by default at loggerheads with each other, at a time when the Maoists and the CPN (UML) were coalition partners in the government. The activities of the Youth Force were 'suspended' in September 2009 while the disbandment of the YCL has one of the main demands of the CPN (UML) and the Nepali Congress. But despite the pressure on the Maoists from many quarters, including international organisations, the UCL remains active and a source of terror for those opposed to it or the Maoists in general. It should be noted though that the YCL is quite inactive in the Tarai, except in certain pockets where the Maoists have a strong presence.

## Current Situation

In July 2009, the government declared that it had identified 109 armed outfits operating in the country, and while all had ostensibly political objectives the modus operandi of many clearly denoted them as being criminal in nature. In the face of growing public criticism, the government's response was to come up with a Special Security Plan (SSP) in July 2009 targeting 27 districts in the Tarai and the eastern hills along with the three in the Kathmandu Valley. But the Plan immediately came under attack from Madhesis, who saw it as specially designed instrument of suppression against the Tarai. A report by a human rights group was blunt in its assessment: Similar attempts by previous governments to address the issue have not had the desired effects; and indeed seem to have resulted in an increase in human rights violations.'[5]

In terms of operations, the SSP has had mixed results. While it has largely been able to prevent blockades of highways by minor groups, targeted assassinations, such as the March 2010 killing of a prominent media entrepreneur in the town of Janakpur and of secretaries of village development committees (VDCs)[6] throughout the Tarai, have highlighted its limited success. Blame for this lies partly with the police itself. As a newspaper report put it: 'The nexus between policemen and criminals for financial gain has been seriously hindering counter-terrorism operations in the central and eastern Tarai.'[7] According to the report, policemen were known to provide information to armed groups and criminal gangs.[8]

A cosy nexus between politician, bureaucrats and criminals exists in the Tarai, and almost everyone admits that armed groups could not have operated without some form of political protection and/or administrative complicity. Local officials complain that when they arrest a 'criminal', politicians immediately call up and exert enormous pressure on them to release the person, claiming that he is in fact their party cadre. In an era of coalitional politics and in the absence of any elected government at the local level, the administration has been working with what are called all-party mechanisms, in which there is representation of all the parties from the district/VDC that received at least 10 per cent of the votes from that area, and that has given considerable clout, without accountability, to political parties. For their part, the politicians assert that it is the police themselves that are involved in promoting these armed groups and criminal gangs in return for a hefty share of the loot extracted through extortion, kidnappings or murder.[9]

There is also the open border with India, the 1700-plus km stretch unregulated for the most part. Citizens of both the countries move freely across the border. Criminal elements on the Nepal side benefit from the easy availability of fire arms on the Indian side, and often taken refuge on the other side after committing a crime in the Tarai. The use of Indian phone lines is common in making extortion or ransom calls. Government officials and businessmen in the Tarai are fearful of answering calls from unknown numbers, fearing an extortion call.

Nepali officials complain that the Indian state turns a blind eye to these activities as long as it does not affect it, and hint that India may be in fact encouraging them. Indian officials dismiss such allegations and cite instances of co-operation; they also blame the Nepali side for not being able to provide any specific intelligence that would allow them to arrest criminals. Observers say that more than the official state apparatus, local Indian politicians and criminals may have helped some of the Madhesi groups in certain instances. But it is also believed that most of the petty crimes such as extortion are the handiwork of Nepali criminals while more sophisticated ones like kidnappings are done by Indian criminals using Nepali partners in crime. Since the region most affected by the armed groups borders northern Bihar, a common view in the Tarai is also that with the improvement in the security situation in Bihar criminal elements from there have found in the Tarai, a fertile ground for their activities.

There is an ongoing process of dialogue with the armed groups, and a number of agreements have been reached with some of these. This has led to the criticism that the government is providing legitimacy to unknown groups and in the process encouraging the emergence of more such entities since amnesty for all crimes is implicit in any agreement with the government.

Ultimately, however, it is the people in the Tarai who are bearing the brunt. Given the centuries of outright discrimination Madhesis have faced, it was natural that any group standing up to the state on their behalf would receive popular support of one form or the other. There was also some measure of acceptance for the targeting of Pahadis in the Tarai, but with the latter having left the southern belt of the Tarai in large numbers, especially the wealthier ones, the armed groups have now turned on the Madhesis themselves in pursuit of their criminal actions.

The political climate has been fragile in the Tarai for almost three full years now. But the government has proved itself completely incompetent in dealing with the situation in the Tarai. The Madhesi political parties that were sent to the constituent assembly in considerable strength have proved themselves incapable of providing a solution, busy as they are in the endless political games in the centre. This has led to serious erosion in the state's credibility in the Tarai.

## NOTES

1. International Crisis Group, 'Nepal's Troubled Tarai Region', 9 July 2007.
2. Nepal is divided in 75 administrative districts.
3. United Nations Office of the High Commissioner for Human Rights in Nepal, 'Allegations of Human Rights Abuses by the Young Communist League (YCL)', June 2007.
4. www.nepalnews.com/main/index.php/news-archive/2-poltical/1357-uml-suspends-yuoSFJKA
5. Advocacy Forum, 'Torture and Extrajudicial Executions amid widespread violence in the Terai', 2010.
6. The lowest administrative unit in Nepal.
7. Sundar Khanal, 'Cop-criminal nexus hinders anti-terror drive', *Republica*, 29 April, 2010.
8. In June 2010, the deputy police chief of Janakpur was suspended for protesting criminals. www.ekantipur.com/the-kathmandu-post/2010/06/21/nation/newsline/209666
9. See, for example, Prashant Jha, 'The centre can't hold'. www.nepalitimes.com.np/issue/2009/02/27/PlainASpeaking/15702

ANNEXURE

**Social Cleavages**

| **Group** | **Remarks** | **Group** | **Remarks** |
|---|---|---|---|
| Madhesis Mountains | Are of Tarai origin | Pahadis | Originally from the Hills, |
| Ethnic groups (Janajatis) | Includes many who live in the Tarai | Caste groups | Includes most Madhesi groups |
| Tarai Janajatis | Are discriminated against by Pahadis but would not like to be limped together with Madhesis, who are also considered interlopers in the Tarai | Madhesis (Tarai caste groups) | Would like to include the Tarai Janajatis into their fold to bolster their numbers |
| Dalits | | Upper castes, including Janajatis | Although most Janajatis do not fall within the caste categories, they equally discriminate against Dalits |
| Religious minorities (Muslims, Christians) | Since the vast majority of Muslims are from the Tarai, they are also identified as Muslims | Hindus/ Buddhists | Most Buddhists would claim they are discriminated against as well. |

**Note:** The divide between Madhesis along caste lines—*Dalits vs Backward Castes vs Upper Castes*—has become more salient over the years.

# 9

# *The Role of Academics in Combating Terrorism: A Closer Look at Bangladesh*

*Imtiaz Ahmed*

Academics are not only part of civil society engaged in reproducing social capital but are also the key actors for recovering, nurturing and disseminating trust, consent and tolerance in the society. The question that needs to be asked then is: Have the academics remained true to their vocation? Or to put it slightly differently, what happens when the academics cross boundaries or when the curtain or *hijab* is lifted and the academics are seen as profiting or becoming indistinguishable from the coercive elements of political society or the economic power of the market? How do their strategic compromises with actors and agencies of both coercive and economic powers, contribute to the business of reproducing terrorism? What role must the academics then play to combat terrorism? The paper will take up this issue in detail.

Let me begin by stating the place of *academics* in the state. After all, we are living in the post-colonial and somewhat post-Westphalian state, and since the 'withering of the state' is still an ideological persuasion, if not too early a call, making the state the focal point of an enquiry into the role of academics in combating terrorism remains a but justifiable proposition. From a methodological standpoint and that would imply without having physical divisions as such, the division the state into three. The first is *political society*, which includes the actors and agencies possessing coercive power. Government, military, police, laws and regulations, and the like, would all come under this sphere.

The second sphere is the *market* or those with economic power. The entire vocation of business or moneymaking falls within this domain. In certain circumstances, this sphere could possess enormous power, indeed, to the point of becoming the determining factor in reproducing or as the case may be, *de-producing* the state. Bangladesh is a good example of this. Critics maintain that just 6-8 importers control 60-80 per cent of all imports of Bangladesh.[1] If this is the case, it is not difficult to understand the enormous profitability of having a political-business nexus for ensuring a super monopoly, whose other name, of course, is corruption.

The third and last sphere is *civil society* or a grouping engaged in the business of reproducing consent or social capital. This would include academics, students, intellectuals, civil rights groups, the media, cultural bodies, sports clubs and other associations; in fact, all the actors and agencies engaged in reproducing social capital in the society. It may be mentioned that in addition to intellectual discourses and social networking or *adda* as we call it 'trust' is a key element for reproducing social capital. Bangladesh fortunately has it in abundance, and this is corroborated not only by national surveys[2] but also by the very fact that the birthplace of micro-credit, which is essentially founded on the principle of trust, happens to be Bangladesh.

Academics, therefore, are not only part of civil society engaged in reproducing social capital but also are among the key actors when it comes to recovering, nurturing and disseminating trust, consent and tolerance in the society. The question that needs to be asked then is: have the academics remained true to their vocation? Or to put it slightly differently, what happens when the academics cross the boundaries or when the curtain or *hijab* is removed and the academics start profiting or become indistinguishable from the coercive elements of political society or the economic power of the market? How do they then stoop to make strategic compromises with actors and agencies of both coercive and economic powers, leading them in turn to contribute in many ways to the business of reproducing terrorism? But before responding to such queries, let me take recourse to Gandhi as a basis for my queries.

Gandhi, while being interviewed by an American journalist, once remarked that there is no caste system in India! How did the old man come to this, what many would regard as, outlandish, conclusion? Gandhi's logic was impeccable as the following conversation with the journalist would show:

> *What about the Brahmans? Asked the journalist.*
>
> "Brahmans were supposed to provide knowledge but today they are busy making money, so there are no Brahmans."

*What about the Ksatriyas?*

"The Ksatriyas were supposed to protect the country but today the British are ruling us, so there are no Ksatriyas."

*What about the Vaisyas?*

"The Vaisyas were supposed to trade honourably but today they are engaged in unfair trading practices, so there are no Vaisyas."

*Surely, then you would agree that there are Sudras?*

"The Sudras were supposed to do menial jobs with the full dignity of a person but today that is not the case. They have been robbed of their dignity, so there are no Sudras!"[3]

In our case, extending the logic would imply that there are no *academics* of merit engaged in reproducing social capital in the highly politicised, polarised, partisan Bangladesh! This, of course, is only partially true and would apply to only some self-willed if not self-aggrandising academics, but let me reflect on the complex nature of things, particularly in relation to the issue of combating terrorism and the role of academics.

There are two sides to the problem when it comes to theorising the relationship between terrorism and the academics. One is *structural* and the other is *intellectual*, although one feeds on the other. Let me reflect on the structural first.

Firstly, *academics as party-demics*. On the surface this seems to be an exercise of democratic rights and ought not to cause any problem. But then our post-independence experience has shown that such academics have mostly ended up in the business of promoting party politics, or worse, partisanship within academic institutions. Dhaka University is a classical case and the 1973 University Order, albeit with some progressive content, is partly responsible for this. The Order, in fact, brought 'elections' into the corridors of the university by introducing a novel system wherein the vice chancellor is 'elected' by the faculty members and other 'elected'/'selected' members of society. It may be mentioned that even Mujib was sceptical about this novelty, telling Kamal Hossain, the then law minister, "Can the teachers handle all these elections?" His scepticism or should we say, fear was well founded. The academics, in fact, over the years have turned into *party-demics* not only for allowing the government into the corridors of the institution but also for succumbing to the government, which true to its 'governmentality' prefers to keep the academics within its fold. This the government succeeded in doing in two ways. First by conflating the responsibility of the state with the responsibility of the government, and making the annual budgetary provisions to public universities the sole discretion of the government. Secondly, and more nakedly, the regime in power became the key actor in appointing the academics both within and outside the university in academically and financially rewarding jobs.

Given such a structure the academics could not help joining the rat race of seeking favour of the party-in -power or for that matter the party-in-waiting. When this happens the academics become hostage to party bosses and cadres, which incidentally includes ideologists, fanatic supporters, even musclemen and *mastans* or petty terrorists, and the vocation of reproducing social capital gets compromised to the point of making *party politics* the means and ends of academic life. And as in national politics, where alliances and numbers play a critical role in strengthening one's constituency, the academics when required, do not hesitate to shake hands and even conspiring with forces colluding with religio-centred extremism! I will have more to say about this shortly.

Secondly, *academics as business-academics*. This cannot be helped. The meagre salaries in public universities either force the academics to take up part-time jobs in private institutions and in the process turn the latter into a full-time and the former into a part-time profession or makes them enter into business—family or fresh. My concern here is not so much with the first, although it is true that the academics in such cases are neither here nor there and as a result their intellectual pursuits suffer. I am more concerned about the business-academics. The latter, in fact, in their zeal to outshine in the business as much as they have done in academics make them fall prey to the political-business nexus and as a result are found hopelessly unable to carry out their primary responsibility of reproducing social capital. With time and economic exigencies they too end up becoming partisan and if a greater volume of primitive accumulation or super profit is promised by the forces colluding with religio-centred extremism then the prospect of a diabolical nexus of the political, business and the academic in the service of religio-centered extremism becomes all the more a living reality. And therein lies the fear.

Finally, *academics as academic-terrorists*. We already have a few of them and some are awaiting jail terms. Terrorism after all is first and foremost an intellectual exercise, only later does it manifest itself as violence. However, the complicity of the state, particularly the activities of some of the actors and agencies within the government, cannot be ruled out for the birth of academic-terrorists. The police interrogation of *mastans* and former ministers now incarcerated, as reported in the media, practically validates this contention. At the same time, it validates the fearful presence of the diabolical nexus of the political, business and the academic that we have referred to earlier. But when does an academic turn into an academic-terrorist? A quick answer would be in the form of a dialectic: *the structural infects the intellectual while the intellectual reproduces the structural.* Let me explain.

Broadly, there are two categories of intellectuals, including academics. The organic or those who are organically connected to the regime or social class and the, dissenters or the revolutionary or those who disown their class and challenge the status quo. Both owe their early conceptualisations to the imprisoned Italian communist, Antonio Gramsci.[4] What is important, however, in contemporary times is, not so much, how they differ in class affiliations, which is what Gramsci was most concerned with, but rather what they are actually advocating and the manner in which they want to accomplish it. But let us return to the question already raised, when does an academic turn into an academic-terrorist? My observations would be limited to the Islamic domain, but the argument could be extended to other religious communities as well.

*Mediocrity* is an undeniable factor when it comes to the issue of religio-centred terrorism within the Islamic domain. There is little doubt that the academic-terrorists have been informed and infected by a rigid or more appropriately ill-informed version of Islam, which in the South Asian or Bangladesh case could be referred to as the Wahhabisation or Salafisation of Islam. It may be mentioned that in pre-colonial times the inter-*mazhab* relationship was more cordial without one trying to dominate the other. I need not go into a detailed discourse regarding the latter except to point out that the interpretation of Islam in South Asia, including Bangladesh, is no longer in the hands of the meritorious but rather for centuries, indeed, partly for reasons of having Muslim despots and partly because of colonial domination, is in the hands of the mediocre. Put differently, the academics have miserably failed to contain rigidities or extremism not so much for the want of motive as for the want of Islamic scholarship.

*Mediagenics* or the love for media attention would be the second factor. Ideally, the academics, particularly at the tertiary level, were supposed to *publish or perish*! But if you have a mediocre academic or an academic who has become lethargic and turned mediocre for reasons of institutional dysfunctionalities it is likely that the person would opt for the 'publish not, perish not' policy. But how does one accomplish that? One way would be to become an academic-terrorist, which would of course include doing terrible things and becoming a leader overnight! Put differently, and to give a prominent example, Professor Ghalib is not known for his intellectual excellence but rather for his advocacy of violence and extremism.[5] Who would have known him otherwise!

Finally, *mechanicality*. Warnings against humans turning into a robots or machines have given many; including Freud, Weber, Tolstoy, Tagore, and a host of other thinkers. Shashi Tharoor, the former Indian under secretary general of the UN, is part of this group but then he is more relevant to the discussion at hand. As Tharoor attempts to answer the not-so pleasing coincidence, *why some engineers become terrorists*:

> Disturbing new research at Oxford University by sociologists Diego Gambetta and Steffen Hertog points to an intriguing—one might say worrying—correlation between engineering and terrorism.... [Consider] the evidence: Osama bin Laden was a student of engineering. So were the star 9/11 kamikaze pilots Mohammed Atta, the alleged mastermind of that plot, Khalid Sheikh Mohammed, and their all-but-forgotten predecessor, the chief plotter of the 1993 World Trade Centre bombing, Ramzi Yousef.
>
> The Oxford scholars, after putting together educational biographies for some 300 known members of violent Islamist groups from 30 countries, concluded that a majority of these Islamist terrorists were not just highly educated, but a startling number of them are engineers. Indeed, according to Gambetta and Hertog, nearly half had studied engineering.
>
> Is there something about engineering that makes its most proficient graduates vulnerable to the temptations of violent extremism? Gambetta and Hertog seem to think so. They have no patience for the more conventional possible explanation — that engineers might be sought after by terrorist groups for their technical expertise in making and blowing up things. Instead, they argue that the reason there are so many terrorist engineers is that the subject helps produce a mindset that makes one prone to radicalisation.[6]

But this need not be limited to engineering. In fact, it can be broadened further and blamed on a mindset nurtured much earlier when one gets to learn 2+2=4, without questioning who is this two? If it is Bush and bin Laden then we could end up having a thousand or more! A comprehensive education, whether secular or religious, is what is missing in the academic of modern times, and 'intellectual certainty' or intolerance has come to roost while *disciplining* the minds in the name of education.

Mediocrity, mediagenics and mechanicality are, of course, as much intellectual as they are structural, all prone to a religio-centered extremism in the business of terrorising the state and the public alike. The current menacing circle therefore has to be broken if a more positive role in combating terrorism is to be expected from academics. Let me then conclude by raising the question, what is to be done?

Counter-terrorism strategy requires a creative inter-play of four Is. The first is *incarceration* or what is commonly referred to as the business of the policing of terrorism by the state. Often there has been an over-emphasis on this strategy, indeed, to a point where the state itself has ended up being 'terroristic'! As Arundhati Roy once pointed out, "There is no terrorism like state terrorism." The excesses of the respective states in Kashmir, Baluchistan, northern Sri Lanka, including 'death in custody' or 'crossfire killing' in Bangladesh are good examples of this. The state, no doubt, would continue to use its coercive power against all possible forms of acts of terror but there is now a serious realisation that this alone cannot contain terrorism. The hanging of six JMB leaders and the continuing threat the terrorist outfit poses is a good example in this context.

The second 'i' is *intelligence.* That intelligence agencies are statist and modelled on 19th century or at the most 20th century requirements and are ill-equipped to tackle the non-state threats of the 21st century is a criticism that is worth examining. But then there are other considerations as well. For instance, we seldom take note of the fact that intelligence agencies are run by human beings, and as such they are liable to get infected with ideas and goals that may not border on tolerance or even match the aspirations of the majority community. Lieutenant Colonel Oliver North and the Iran-Contra affair is a good example, as is the case of Lieutenant Colonel Prasad Shrikant Purohit or more blatantly, if we are to believe some of the reports that come out in the media, the role of the CIA, Scotland Yard, MI16, ISI, RAW or DGFI. Given this scenario, there is an urgent need to re-invent the domain of intelligence. Since the threat under discussion is the non-state, it is important that civilians are engaged creatively in this domain.

The academics have certainly less to do with the above two 'i'-s, that is, incarceration and intelligence. It is the third 'i'—*intellectual*—that is central to the academics and here they have a more direct role to play in combating terrorism. Indeed, the intellectual intervention needs to be geared up, and in this the Bangladeshi academics are slightly blessed! Bengal, after all, is the domain of the tolerant Sufis and the relatively more receptive (juristic) tradition of the Hanafis. There is therefore immense hope, despite the fact that the latter, including Sufism with its contradictory admixture of Sufi + ism,[7] has lately been infected by the more rigid creed or Wahhabism. The problem, to be more precise, is one of dogma and is related to, as Fatema Mernissi points out, the 'Muslim's duty to turn into a rebel against an imam (leader) who makes unjust decisions.'[8] Over the years two opposing traditions have emerged. One, that of the intolerant and often blood thirsty Kharijites, while the other the rationalist Mutazila, both differing in terms of the means to be employed in the rebellion but sharing 'one basic idea: the imam must be modest and must in no way turn to despotism.'[9] But then, over the years if the Mutazila were condemned and systematically driven out or exterminated by Muslim despots, the Kharijites re-created themselves in the midst of newer despots and those championing the cause of extremism, including Wahhabism. Are the academics of contemporary times equipped to confront the latter that has by now infected the Muslim mind and made it relatively more intolerant and violent? Or, are they uncomfortable with the prospect of recovering the Mutazila and restoring its place in Islam, which could have the effect of delinking them from the (despotic) state and losing its much-coveted favour?

Lack of religious knowledge need not be blamed for all the intolerance and extremism in the Muslim community. This we have referred to earlier while highlighting the correlation between engineering and violent extremism. Moreover, critics at the University of Chicago's *Project on Suicide Terrorism* found no relationship between suicide terrorism and education, not even with country's wealth and level of terrorism.[10] In fact, the Chicago study, looking at the beliefs of 384 of the 462 suicide attackers in the period between 1980 and 2003, found that 43 per cent were religious and 57 per cent secular. If those whose ideology could not be determined and were assumed to be religiously motivated then it would bring the religious group to 52 per cent.[11] The evidence is more towards ideological drives and group dynamics, indicating thereby that there are both secular and religious compulsions for reproducing violent extremism. In the case of Bangladesh, therefore, there is an urgent need for the academics to intensify critical research and reflections and not engage themselves in a priori formulations and politically soothing conclusions. The former would certainly help reproduce social capital while the latter would only serve the coercive and ill-bred economic forces.

Certain *institutional* innovations are however required to make space for academics to ponder and pursue the intellectual, and this brings us to the fourth and last 'i'. I will limit myself to three. Firstly, 'racial politics' in public universities, including Dhaka University, must come to an end. I am of course referring to the party-demics and their obsession with party politics and partisanship. In fact, once I saw an interesting slogan on the wall of the vice chancellor's residence in Dhaka University: *bornabad nipat jak* (down with racism)! Somewhat puzzled, I told my students that it gives me pleasure to see such writings on the wall and the interest of the students' community in problems affecting the United States and South Africa. My students quickly corrected me: "But, sir, it is a call to shun the blue-white-pink politics of the teachers!" Party-demics only create space for mastans and petty terrorists, a role model hardly conducive to the reproduction of trust and social capital.

A double-layered delinking is required for the role of academics to be meaningful in combating terrorism. Firstly, the autonomy of public universities must be fully restored and this can come about by ending the current system of appointing the academics to keys posts in the university. What is required are independent (national or international) search committees and that again for a fixed period of time. Secondly, the delinking of the student bodies from party-demics and party politics. I must quickly add here that this should not be understood as doing away with the student unions. On the contrary, the students and the student unions need to be salvaged from party-demics and party politics and put into the service of reproducing social capital.

The second institutional innovation relates to regional/global security. It is already in the air that the Europeans are in the final stage of establishing a Counter-Terrorism Centre (CTC) in Bangladesh. There are good reasons for the government of Bangladesh to have approved such a centre. In fact, the current regime under the leadership of Sheikh Hasina has mooted the idea of establishing a South Asian Task Force to contain and counter-terrorism. It may be pointed out that Bangladesh probably is the only country in the world where both the president and the prime minister suffered directly from terrorist attacks. The president's wife, Ivy Rahman, was killed while Sheikh Hasina's hearing was damaged by terrorist attacks, which many believe were meant to kill her. In such a scenario, it is quite natural for the current regime to remain extra-attentive and open to newer institutions, including CTC, when it comes to countering terrorism. And it is here that the academics have a potential role to play. In fact, if the CTC is to have a constant yet independent flow of information and analysis then it cannot do without a *research cell*, mainly of critical academics, researchers and scholars. The centre, of course, would also require *intelligence* and *media* cells, but without the 'information' from both these cells getting critically and independently researched the concerned members would not be able to judge the character of the crisis and recommend unbiased policy options for resolving it.

The final institutional innovation relates to disseminating the intellectual input of the academic to the public and beyond the corridors of the institution. In certain respect, the days of armchair academics are over! Workshops, seminars, dialogues, poster campaigns, column writings, and the like, while reproducing social capital, go a long way towards highlighting the menace and the need for combating terrorism. Here I must quickly add that my little experience in researching on terrorism has made me realise the effectiveness of the visual medium in highlighting the impact of terrorism. I soon discovered this when I ventured to produce a documentary on the victims of small arms and explosives with the full support of my students, from directing, acting to filming.[12] Participants after watching the documentary were found to be more attentive about the subject and were receptive to the idea of doing something noble for the victims. This would imply that academics and academic institutions, if they are to have a role in combating terrorism, must now turn to the visual medium by way of having their own television channels. This goal may sound a little bit far-fetched at this moment, but it is not beyond the realm of possibility, at least in some universities in South Asia, including Dhaka University in Bangladesh. In fact, academics must make sure that they are *heard* and *seen* if they are to seek the support of the public in combating terrorism.

## NOTES

1. M.A. Rouf Chowdhury, "Wake Up! A New Bangladesh Knocks On Your Door." Paper presented at the *Dialogue on Bangladesh Economy & Future Perspective*, Ministry of Commerce, Government of Bangladesh, 5 September 2007, Radisson Water Garden Hotel, Dhaka.
2. For a closer exposition of the higher degree of 'trust' in Bangladesh compared to other South Asian countries, see, *State of Democracy in South Asia: A Report*, edited by SDSA Team (New Delhi: Oxford University Press, 2008).
3. Mahatma Gandhi, *The Moral and Political Writings of Mahatma Gandhi*, Volume II; Edited by Raghavan Narasimhan Iyer (Oxford: Clarendon Press, 1986).
4. Antonio Gramsci, *Selections from the Prison Notebooks* (New York: International Publishers, 1971).
5. Dr. Muhammad Asadullah al-Ghalib, a professor of Arabic Studies at Rajshahi University, is also a top leader in the JMB as well as the chief of another radical Islamist organisation, *Ahle Hadith Andolon Bangladesh* (AHAB). As chief of AHAB, which is "a mass platform for JMB activities, al-Ghalib was running a magazine, *Al-Tahreek*. Al-Ghalib was arrested in February 2005. He was charged with sedition at a northwestern Natore District court, along with 14 others. See, Adam E. Stahl, "Jama'atul Mujahideen Bangladesh: Militant Islamist Terror," International Institute for Counter Terrorism, 30 April, 2007, www.ict.org.il
6. *The Times of India*, 30 March 2008.
7. There is a qualitative difference between being a Sufi and *Sufism*. The latter, like any other *ideological* quest, either of earlier or of contemporary times, is increasingly turning conformist, which is certainly contrary to its original advocacy of non-conformism and freethinking. For details, see, Imtiaz Ahmed, *Sufis and Sufism: The journey of the Sufis from the Middle East to Bangladesh* (Singapore: Middle East Institute, National University of Singapore, 2010).
8. Fatema Mernissi, *Islam and Democracy: Fear of the Modern World* (New York: Basic Books, 2002), p. 27.
9. Ibid., p. 33.
10. Robert Pape, *The Chicago Project on Suicide Terrorism*, University of Chicago, 2005, http://jtac.uchicago.edu/conferences/05/resources/pape_formatted%20for%20DTRA.pdf
11. Ibid.
12. The title of the documentary: *small arms are no longer small*, produced by Centre for Alternatives, February 2008.

# SECTION II

# Regional Cooperation in Counter-terrorism

# 10

# *Opportunities for Regional Stability: The View from Pakistan*

*Shehryar Fazli*[1]

## Introduction

Pakistan-based militant groups with a proven ability to strike at home, in India, and beyond, and with demonstrable links to international terrorist networks pose the most significant threat to stability in South Asia. The current domestic and international focus on extremist groups in the Federally Administered Tribal Areas (FATA), while understandable, has resulted in inadequate efforts being made against, radical Sunni groups based in the Pakistani heartland, who are in fact significantly more dangerous than their FATA-based counterparts. Taking credible action against them should be a top domestic and international priority. While Pakistan's elected government has pledged that it will not allow its territory to be used for attacks on foreign soil, its success in so doing will depend on political stability and a sustained democratic transition at home that enables the political leadership to wrest control over key domestic and foreign policy—including security and the India policy—and a justice sector that has the capacity to dismantle extremist organisations and investigate and convict their members. The same challenges apply to other South Asian states, including India. Regional efforts to counter-terrorism should build on the SAARC Convention on Mutual Legal Assistance in Criminal Matters by prioritising enhancement of civilian law enforcement and prosecution agencies, rather the current over-reliance on military action which has produced few long-term results.

At the end of 2008, Pakistan had experienced its worst year of terrorist attacks. 2009 proved even worse, and 2010 could turn out to be bloodier still. Casualties from terrorist violence in Pakistan now outpace both Iraq and Afghanistan. The army operations against militant networks in Khyber Pakhtunkwa's (KPK's) Malakand region, and in the Federally Administered Tribal Areas (FATA) bordering Afghanistan, have provoked mass displacement, civilian casualties, destruction to infrastructure and shattered local economies, while counter-insurgency successes have been at best limited. While Malakand-based militant groups do not operate as openly as they did before the launch of military operations there in May 2009, they remain intact, none of their leaders have been convicted, and their attacks on the state and citizenry continue. The July 2010 floods, causing enormous damage to KPK, as elsewhere, have added to the challenges, particularly as jihadi groups try to exploit public grievances and win constituents by carrying out relief activities. These outfits not only pose a regional threat, with a demonstrated capacity to strike in India and Afghanistan, but indeed global one.

Yet, if these groups have the ability to strike within the region and beyond, there is broad recognition in Pakistan that they pose first and foremost a threat to the Pakistani state and citizen. Particularly since the Malakand crisis, more and more segments of the public are exhausted by conflict, rejecting extremism and demanding rule of law—even, or especially, in the most socially conservative areas that have been hit the hardest. At the same time, an albeit fragile democratic transition continues. The Pakistan People's Party's (PPP's) planned economic reforms have been stalled due to opposition in parliament, including plans to raise fuel prices and for a Reformed General Sales Tax (RGST) bill, while the party holds on to a tenuous coalition. Nevertheless, the major political parties achieved important milestones in 2010 to reinforce parliamentary supremacy and provincial autonomy, and remove the constitutional distortions of the previous military government.

The elected leadership has also repeatedly expressed a desire to achieve sustainable peace with its neighbours. Before the 2008 Mumbai attacks, the PPP-led government was committed to the composite dialogue with New Delhi that began in 2004, and continues to support its resumption. Another Mumbai-like attack, however, would have a devastating impact on Pakistan-India relations, possibly provoking a military confrontation, or at least the prospect of one, as occurred after the attack on the Indian parliament in December 2001. This would seriously set back efforts to achieve regional stability.

Given the reach of Pakistan-based terrorist groups, and the regional implications, a successful counter-terrorism strategy in Pakistan will be vital to reducing the threat in the region, and could also provide policy direction for

Pakistan's neighbours, as well as arguably the most influential actor in the region, the U.S. So far, with the U.S. still focused on militancy in the tribal belt bordering Afghanistan, its primary partner remains the Pakistani military. However, as this paper will argue, the most significant threat comes not from the FATA-based networks but those operating in the heartland, running training camps, mosques and madrasas (still key places of jihadi recruitment and indoctrination) from one side of the country to the other. If Pakistan-based militants do execute another Mumbai-like attack in India, or even beyond the region, they are far more likely to belong to one of these groups than the so-called Pakistani Taliban. This paper will examine the challenge in Pakistan's heartland, and propose a new, civilian-led approach for Islamabad, as well as international and regional actors, with particular focus on steps that the Indian and Pakistani governments can take to alleviate mistrust, empower moderate forces on both sides, and contain the spread of religious extremism.

## Diagnosing the Problem

A common explanation for the spread of violence in Pakistan is that militancy in FATA has become so rampant that it has spilled over into other parts of the country, including Punjab. The term 'Punjabi Taliban' has been gaining currency of late. Yet, if it alludes to the very real problem of terrorism in Pakistan's most populous province, the term also suggests that this problem remains primarily a Pashtun one, which begins in the tribal belt and, because of its enormous growth, is spilling south. The logical conclusion is that if we tackle the monster in FATA, we can perhaps cut it off at its head, thus containing the crisis in the rest of the country, and indeed the region. There is, therefore, considerable domestic and international attention and support to the military's operations against the loose alliance of FATA-based groups commonly referred to as the Pakistani Taliban, or TTP.

Hence, when an attack occurs in major cities like Lahore or Islamabad, the gut reaction from officials and the press is usually that the Waziristan-based Mehsuds are responsible. This is a misdiagnosis, often exposed during the course of investigations that invariably reveal one or other of the Sunni sectarian groups that have been operating in Punjab since the 1980s. The September 2008 Marriott attack is emblematic: on the day of the attack, the interior minister (then a government adviser) Rehman Malik said that "all roads lead to Waziristan",[2] even as investigators suggested that the attack was coordinated by a Punjab-based group. Acknowledging this, Malik later attributed the Marriott bombing to the Punjab-based radical Sunni Lashkar-e-Jhangvi (LeJ). This pattern was repeated in later attacks, such as the one on the Sri Lankan cricket team in

Lahore and the Lahore police academy in early 2009—each time, the press and government and military officials pin the blame on a Waziristan-based tribal boogieman: today, Hakimullah Mehsud, before him Baitullah Mehsud and, in earlier years of the conflict, one Nek Mohammed.[3] Each time, the investigations point not to the TTP but to central or southern Punjab. With the recent targeted killings of Ahmadis in Lahore, articles and editorials appear finally to be focusing on the internal threat from groups like the LeJ, its parent Sipah-e-Sahaba (SSP) and the Jaish-e-Mohammad, but few identify them as the epicenter of militancy in Pakistan.[4]

It is worthwhile recalling that sectarian violence remains the primary source of terrorism in the country, and the continued attacks on religious and sectarian minorities not just in the old hotspots of Karachi and southern Punjab, but also in large parts of KPK, FATA and Balochistan's provincial capital, Quetta, demonstrate that the pattern hasn't changed so much as assumed far greater proportions. The LeJ and parent SSP now have major bases in FATA's Orakzai and Kurram Agencies, where Sunni-Shia conflict continues to escalate and paralyze everyday life. Such groups supply networks in the tribal belt with a vital source of recruits, commanders, financing, material resources and intelligence. LeJ members are even seconded to KPK and FATA to serve as leaders of local TTP chapters. These outfits also have demonstrable links to international terrorist networks like al-Qaeda.[5]

What ramifications does this have for a successful Pakistani, and regional, counter-terrorism strategy? Notwithstanding the occasional comment by some state official or other, a 'Swat-like' military operation in southern Punjab is neither likely nor desired. If the groups that pose the biggest threat to Pakistan and its neighbours are operating in the heartland, rather than in the borderlands of the northwest, then a shift in focus is urgently needed from a military to a civilian-led counter-terrorism effort. Unfortunately, after eight years of military rule, Pakistan's civilian law enforcement agencies lack resources, investigative capacity and the necessary political backing. During the Pervez Musharraf regime, the courts were weakened further. The general conviction rate is around 5 to 10 per cent—in terrorism cases, even lower. Nevertheless, when properly equipped and authorised, civilian law enforcement agencies have achieved notable successes. In the late 1990s, for example, when sectarian terrorism was threatening to destabilize the state, civilian agencies were instrumental in countering the Sipah-e-Sahaba, compelling the organisation to vacate its main base in Punjab and relocate to Afghanistan.[6] Police also busted major kidnapping gangs in Karachi, which have a strong connection to extremist networks. Although the terrorist rot goes significantly deeper today than it did in the 1990s, the solution remains the same: strengthening the civilian law enforcement apparatus, including police, prosecutors, and courts.

## Building Capacity

The investigation and prosecution services are understaffed and starved of financial and material resources. Investigation and forensics, evidence gathering, and witness protection, are so limited that prosecutors end up relying on forced confessions, which are inadmissible in court, and the main reason why cases are dismissed. Moreover, civilian officials face political barriers to accessing vital data, such as mobile phone records (often the starting point of an investigation), which are obtained only through the military's intelligence agencies. Until the authority and the capacities of national and provincial institutions and agencies to counter-terrorism are enhanced, the prospects for meaningful regional cooperation will be limited at best.

There is indeed appetite for reform in Pakistan. There are strong proponents of enhancing the criminal justice system in parliament—government and opposition—as well as in the police service itself. There are also efforts underway to gain greater civilian ownership over counter-terrorism. A parliamentary committee in the National Assembly, for example, has raised the issue of the police's lack of direct access to mobile phone data. The Shahbaz Sharif-led Punjab government, too, has taken some major initiatives, including for the establishment of a large-scale forensics lab with DNA analysis, toxicology, bomb site investigation capabilities, and other essentials, with scientists trained in the U.S. and elsewhere.[7]

Yet, the challenge in Pakistan's current democratic transition is for the major political parties to be able to implement their policy preferences by wresting control over counter-terrorism and foreign policy, and for weak civilian institutions to achieve the capacity to enforce policy and law. While this is primarily a Pakistani responsibility, other countries can play a critical role. To do so, they need to think beyond military-to-military relations, understand that successful counter-terrorism will be civilian-led, and shift the focus to institutions like the investigation and prosecution agencies. Even when India and Pakistan did start sharing intelligence post-Mumbai, under auspices of the CIA, the cooperation is typically with the military's intelligence agencies. Where the U.S. has facilitated intelligence sharing between India and Pakistan, in a bid to defuse tensions, it has again focused primarily on militants in the northwest, and the Pakistani military's operations against them.[8]

Meanwhile, an anti-terrorism court is conducting proceedings against Zakiur Rehman Lakhvi, a LeT leader, and six others accused of planning the Mumbai attacks. This is in itself significant because it is the first time that the state has charged anyone for a terrorist attack on foreign soil. The convictions of the planners of the Mumbai attacks in credible trials would promote deeper trust between the two governments, not to mention the public. On the other hand, the trial will lose its significance if the courts do not convict those responsible in these or any subsequent proceedings. Since August 2010, the Pakistani government has been urging India for access to two witnesses that it believes would be crucial to obtaining a conviction—so far, without success.

The imperative of building the capacities of civilian law enforcement agencies is not uniquely a Pakistani one. In the aftermath of the Mumbai attacks, India, too, has acknowledged weaknesses in its prosecution and investigation services, and is taking steps to address them,[9] as are other South Asia states. The SAARC Convention on Mutual Legal Assistance in Criminal Matters (2008), with its focus on investigations and prosecutions, rightly recognizes the need to "strengthen regional cooperation in the fight against cross-border crimes, in particular the fight against terrorism"[10] through the criminal justice systems of the states.[11]

The challenges in implementing the Convention became apparent a few months after it was adopted in 2008, with the Mumbai attacks in November, and the insufficient cooperation between the two governments in bringing the perpetrators to justice, as noted above. There has been ample reporting on SAARC's limitations due to the state of India-Pakistan relations. Yet, with Islamabad and New Delhi both recognizing the importance of their criminal justice sectors, they could alleviate some of the post-Mumbai mistrust if they seized the opportunity to identify and build on common needs, including investigation and collection of evidence in terrorism and other criminal cases that implicate actors on both sides; share intelligence through, for example, maintaining shared databases of suspects; and being more cooperative in providing witnesses and other material necessary to the prosecution of culprits, under the terms of the SAARC Convention.

After their meeting in Islamabad in June 2010, home ministers from the SAARC states pledged to enhance intelligence-sharing, and Pakistan has proposed a regional institution modeled on Interpol.[12] Joint training of investigators and prosecutors from the member states, focusing on evidence gathering and case building, should also be considered, and would not be as politically charged as cooperation between militaries or their intelligence agencies. Any such solution will only be as good as each state's counter-terrorism capacity. In Pakistan, where the terrorist threat keeps expanding but where civilian law enforcement agencies remain critically under-equipped, the international community at large, particularly the U.S. and EU, should help strengthen civilian institutions rather than circumvent them to collaborate directly with the military, on the grounds of urgent counter-terrorism needs.

The opportunities are there. The international community is finally responding to the necessities of better policing. In 2007, while it provided the military with more than $730 million in aid, the U.S. government provided the police with an almost insignificant $4.9 million. Since then, there have been more concerted international efforts to support Pakistan's police, not just from the U.S., which mentions police reform as a priority in the Enhanced Partnership with Pakistan Act, 2009, or Kerry-Lugar-Berman bill, but also the EU under its Civilian Capacity Building for Law Enforcement in Pakistan (CCBLE). Within the region, Pakistani anti-terrorism units receive training in Indonesia's police academy for its Detachment 88 force, which has scored successes against terrorist networks in that country.[13] In addition to civilian law enforcement agencies, the U.S. and EU are also supporting training and trial advocacy programs for prosecutors. These efforts are welcome, but ultimately reforms to Pakistan's civilian law enforcement agencies, with international support, need to be far more vigorous.

## Political Stability and Regional Peace

Political stability in Pakistan will enable the moderate secular majority and political leadership to assert itself and help improve relations with Pakistan's neighbours. As mentioned above, the democratic transition remains fragile, despite some very significant reforms. While President Asif Ali Zardari has also issued positive signals on reducing tensions with India, his PPP-led government will be unable to put policy into practice unless the transition stabilizes, and domestic and international actors engage with the civilian leadership rather than look for shortcuts through lopsided dealings with the military, which have yielded few long-term counter-terrorism dividends in the last nine years.

By freezing their bilateral relations in response to an event like the Mumbai attacks, Islamabad and New Delhi grant more space to hardliners on both sides, including those who are prepared to use violence to derail dialogue and any steps towards peace in the region. They also lose opportunities to cooperate on vital initiatives like intelligence and evidence sharing between civilian law enforcement agencies. International donors, too, tend to shut down cross-border and cross-Line of Control (LOC) initiatives when tensions rise, such as the Asia Development Bank's planned infrastructure support program for the implementation of CBMs after 2004, which was put on hold after the 2005 earthquake, but also as a result of rising India-Pakistan tensions. Such programs become more important exactly when there is an escalation of conflict.[14] These international organisations, too, are potentially powerful regional actors. What they, and the Indian and Pakistani governments, can achieve in regional cooperation efforts, perhaps above all, is to embolden moderates and create powerful constituencies for peace amongst the public, particularly Kashmiris on both sides of the LOC. Confidence Building Measures (CBMs), including cross border and cross-LOC trade, can indeed produce compelling incentives for peace. The more stakes professional associations and civil society organisations on both sides have in stable India-Pakistan relations, the more able and invested they will be in pressing their respective governments to improve bilateral relations.

In October 2008, New Delhi and Islamabad took the vital step of launching cross-LOC trade, for the first time since independence—but they still control it too tightly. The list of tradable goods, for instance, does not maximize the potential of inter-Kashmir trade since it excludes many goods that could actually have high trade value, while a rigid travel regime, high transportation costs, and restrictions on communications across the LOC that prevents traders from accessing market information, have also severely limited the impact of this significant step.[15]

Cross-LOC interaction should also be expanded beyond trade and current proposals for increased people-to-people contacts, with the state capitals, Muzaffarabad and Sringar, granted greater authority and independence to shape the terms according to their constituents' needs. The recent humanitarian crises in Pakistan—the 2005 earthquake, the IDP crisis in Khyber Pakhtunkwa, and the July 2010 floods—provide new challenges but also opportunities to engage the moderate majority and improve bilateral relations. Many lives, for example, could have been saved in the earthquake's aftermath if villagers in the hardest hit and most remote areas of Azad Kashmir had access to facilities across the LOC.[16] Militant groups are trying to exploit the floods in Pakistan as they did the earthquake and last year's IDP crisis in Malakand. Although the Pakistani public, including in KPK, has rejected religious extremism, the worst affected could become soft targets for jihadi groups if the state and humanitarian community fail to meet their urgent needs.[17]

Writing on the floods, Indian analyst Praful Bidwai argued, "Besides a humanitarian obligation, India has a high stake in such an outcome. India is uniquely placed to quickly deliver foodgrains, clothes, tents, rubber dinghies and other material to Pakistan". Bidwai criticised New Delhi for providing only $25 million at the time.[18] Since then, after the UN revised its appeal for flood relief to $2 billion on 17 September, India responded—the first country to do so—with an additional $25 million. This is encouraging, but a more proactive approach is nevertheless needed, based on mutual interest and broad public engagement, which would limit the ability of militant groups like the Jamaat-ud-Dawa (the renamed LeT) to fill the breach through their charity wings.

Finally, religious hardliners and Pakistan-based extremists could also exploit the currently volatile climate in Jammu and Kashmir. With violence and clashes between protesters and police and security forces escalating in India-administered Kashmir, it is therefore vital that the Indian government respect constitutionally guaranteed Kashmiri human, political and economic rights; repeal laws that give security forces arbitrary powers of arrest, detention and use of force; and carry through on its pledge to hold meaningful dialogue involving a full spectrum of Kashmiri political opinion to end the region's political and economic isolation.

## Conclusion

Regional counter-terrorism efforts will only be as good as the national capacities of individual states to tackle militant networks. The Pakistani and Indian government have both acknowledged the need for a strong law enforcement apparatus to counter the menace of terrorism, and both countries face threats from the same extremists groups, which are bent on spreading a rigid and violent ideology in the region, and intensifying the conflict between these nuclear-armed neighbours. If it is unrealistic to expect a solution to the Kashmir dispute in the short term, more interaction between civilian institutions and the moderate public on both sides can help create the environment for greater cross-border cooperation, including to marginalize religious hardliners and extremists.

With every report of an international terror plot originating in Pakistan, the domestic and international response typically settles on the same solution: more military action in FATA. The dangers of this narrow approach are becoming increasingly clear, as sectarian groups based in the Pakistani heartland like the Lashkar-e-Jhangvi, Jaish-e-Mohammad and Laskhar-e-Tayyeba, become more emboldened, kill Shias and other minorities across the country, and plan attacks in India, Afghanistan and the West. While the elected government in Islamabad has pledged that it will prevent its territory from being used for attacks on foreign soil, its success in doing so will depend on two key things: a sustained democratic transition that enables the political leadership to wrest control over key domestic and foreign policy areas, including security and India policy; and a justice sector that has the capacity to dismantle extremist organisations and investigate and convict their members.

The international community at large should recognize that deviations from the rule of law will make sustainable counter-terrorism successes less likely. The underlying purpose of the Kerry-Lugar-Berman bill is to broaden engagement with Pakistan beyond a narrow relationship with the military. This principle should be reinforced in all assistance programs, including for flood relief, rehabilitation and reconstruction, which often circumvent elected national and provincial assemblies and rely too heavily on unaccountable bureaucracies and the military. New Delhi, too, should appreciate that a successful democratic transition across the border will expand its options in reducing the threat to its own citizens. The post-Mumbai climate could in fact yield a positive change of direction if both governments build on their recognition of the importance of a strong criminal justice to contain extremism in the region. Their cooperation in trials, under the terms of the SAARC Convention on Mutual Legal Assistance in Criminal Matters, supported by broader international efforts to enhance investigation and prosecution capacity in South Asia, is far more likely to achieve regional stability than an over-reliance on a military solution.

## Notes

1. This chapter draws substantially on research the author conducted as a senior analyst for the International Crisis Group.
2. "All roads lead to Waziristan", *Daily Times*, September 22, 2008.
3. Baitullah Mehsud was killed in a U.S. drone strike in August 2009; Nek Mohammad was killed in an American airstrike in June 2004.
4. The Lashkar-e-Tayyeba (LeT), which carried out the Mumbai attacks, is also Punjab-based.
5. For more detail, see "Pakistan: The Militant Jihadi Challenge", International Crisis Group, March 13, 2009.
6. The Nawaz Sharif government sent a high-level delegation to Kabul to press Mullah Omar to extradite SSP and LeJ leaders like Riaz Basra. That dialogue was interrupted when the Sharif was deposed by Pervez Musharraf's coup in October 1999. See ibid.
7. For more detail on this project, see the Punjab Forensic Science Agency website: http://www.pfsa.gop.pk/.
8. See, for example, Jay Solomon and Siobhan Gorman, "Pakistan, India and U.S. begin sharing intelligence", *Wall Street Journal*, May 21, 2009.
9. See Sumit Ganguly, "Counter-terrorism cooperation in South Asia: History and prospects", Special Report #21, National Bureau of Asian Research, December 2009.
10. Media release: "SAARC Convention to help in combating terrorism", Ministry of Foreign Affairs, Government of Sri Lankan, August 27, 2008. http://www.slmission.com/media-releases/21-ministry-media-releases-/123-saarc-convention-to-help-in-combating-terrorism.html
11. It envisions, among other measures, "facilitating the appearance the appearance of witnesses or the assistance of persons in investigations". Article 1.4 (viii), "SAARC Convention on Mutual Legal Assistance in Criminal Matters".
12. See "SAARC Nations Pledge Coordinated Action against Terrorism", Press Trust of India, June 26, 2010.

13. See Hannah Beech, "The Right Might", *Time*, June 7, 2010.
14. See "Steps Towards Peace: Putting Kashmiris First", International Crisis Group, June 3, 2010.
15. Ibid.
16. Ibid.
17. For more detail, see "Pakistan: The Worsening IDP Crisis", International Crisis Group, September 16, 2010.
18. Praful Bidwai, "Natural Calamity and Social Crisis", *Daily Star*, September 6, 2010.

## REFERENCES

"All roads lead to Waziristan", *Daily Times*, September 22, 2008

Hannah Beech, "The right might", *Time*, June 7, 2010.

Praful Bidwai, "Natural calamity and social crisis", *Daily Star*, 6 September, 2010.

Sumit Ganguly, "Counter-terrorism cooperation in South Asia: History and prospects", Special Report #21, National Bureau of Asian Research, December 2009.

Sobhan Gorman and Jay Solomon. "Pakistan, India and U.S. begin sharing intelligence", *Wall Street Journal*, May 21, 2009

International Crisis Group. "Pakistan: The Militant Jihadi Challenge", March 13, 2009.

____. "Steps Towards Peace: Putting Kashmiris First", June 3, 2010.

____, "Pakistan: The Worsening IDP Crisis", September 16, 2010.

"SAARC Convention to help in combating terrorism", Ministry of Foreign Affairs, Government of Sri Lankan, August 27, 2008.

"SAARC Convention on Mutual Legal Assistance in Criminal Matters".

"SAARC nations pledge coordinated action against terrorism", Press Trust of India, June 26, 2010.

# 11

# *Assessing Counter-terror Cooperation in South Asia*

*Anand Kumar*

South Asia has been one of the earliest victims of terrorism. Terrorism was raging in this region in the second half of the 20th century. The nature and the reasons for terrorism varied from country to country. The countries of the region could have overcome this menace if they had chosen to cooperate with each other. Unfortunately, for a long period this cooperation was missing and countries were accused of fuelling terrorism in each other's territory. However, as most countries suffer at the hands of terrorists, it is being increasingly realised that not acting against terror groups will also exact a cost. The states moved to act against terror groups when they realised—the hard way—that if they had to survive they had to cooperate. Now a near consensus seems to be emerging that action should be taken against terrorists through cooperation.

Since India is at the centre of SAARC and is the only country which shares borders with every other member country, counter terror cooperation in South Asia often boils down to cooperation between India and other SAARC nations.

Now the discourse on counter-terrorism has gone beyond establishing the existence of terror groups and their camps in countries. If the action against terror groups by Bhutan and Bangladesh proved their existence, 26/11 and arrest of Ajmal Amir Kasab along with access to David Coleman Headley has conclusively proved that terror groups have been operating from Pakistan. Finally, the statement made by Musharraf that Pakistan created Islamist groups to wage war in Kashmir can now be taken as an official admission. Today, South Asians are faced with three questions—whether to cooperate, how to cooperate or not to cooperate. Thankfully, now a majority of South Asian countries have decided to cooperate and they have also been finding ways to cooperate.

This paper argues that most states in South Asia started cooperating with each other when they realised that terrorism posed a threat to their very existence and the survival of their governments. It may also lead to chaos. However, this cooperation is missing in those cases where governments still think that terror can be harnessed for strategic benefits. This has also been the reason why cooperation on terror at the regional level has not taken off.

## Evolution of Counter-terror Cooperation in South Asia

The last decade of twentieth century was the heyday of the terrorism in South Asia. If it was LTTE in Sri Lanka, then Maoists were fighting the monarchy in Nepal. Similarly terror groups were increasing their presence and activities in India, Bhutan, Bangladesh, Myanmar, Pakistan and Afghanistan.

A turning point in counter-terrorism however came because of an event that took place outside the region. This event was 9/11 which made international community realise that if terrorist groups are allowed to flourish in South Asia then they would not allow the rest of the world to live in peace. The attack on the twin towers not only brought the West into South Asia but it also prompted them to encourage India and Pakistan to cooperate under SAARC and work for peace and progress. The developments at the Islamabad SAARC summit could be taken as starting point in this context. Effort was made to consolidate this development in subsequent SAARC summits. Though these efforts could not significantly bridge the gulf between India and Pakistan they did motivate other nations to cooperate on terror. Most of these countries were themselves under terrorist threat. Besides, international opinion had decisively turned against terrorism.

## Bhutanese Operations

Bhutan undertook military action against Indian insurgent groups under "Operation All Clear" on December 15, 2003 to oust them from its territory. At the time of the operation there were over 3,000 heavily armed Indian separatists belonging to three different groups, the ULFA, NDFB and the KLO based in Bhutan. They were operating from 30 camps inside the kingdom.[1] Out of these, 13 camps belonged to the ULFA, NDFB had 12 while the KLO had five.

The virtually illegal occupation of southern Bhutan by the terrorists posed a serious challenge to its sovereignty. The state had actually started withdrawing from these areas by closing down commercial and other institutions. The terrorists were also hampering economic activities in Bhutan besides affecting its trade and commerce. Work at large industries such as the Dungsum Cement project was suspended. Educational institutions in terrorist-infested areas were closed down. Trade, agriculture production and other commercial activities in several districts of the country were disrupted. Ordinary citizens did not feel free to even travel across the country. Many became victims of threats, coercion and extortion. Unprovoked attacks by the militants against Bhutanese nationals inside the country, as well as those travelling through the Indian state of Assam resulted in the loss of innocent lives.

Before opting for the military operation Bhutan had tried to persuade the insurgents to leave the kingdom peacefully. But after several round of talks spanning over six years, it had become almost certain that the militants had no intention of leaving Bhutan. In all the meetings between Bhutan and the insurgent groups, while Bhutan sent its top officials the insurgents were represented by middle level leaders. Some ULFA leaders even said that leaving Bhutan was as good as bidding goodbye to their cause for which they were not ready.[2]

The Bhutanese king was dithering before taking military action as he was not sure of his military power. Its forces had not been in combat in more than a century. Bhutan also knew that action against the insurgents would make them hostile towards Bhutanese citizens and even Royal Bhutan Army. Most importantly Bhutanese had to travel through Indian territory to reach southern Bhutan.

What tipped the balance against the terrorists and prompted the government to take military action against the militants was the formation of the Bhutan Communist Party (Marxist-Leninist-Maoist) on April 22, 2003.[3] This party wanted to over throw the monarchy and establish a 'true and new democracy' in Bhutan. It was also feared that the KLO was in league with the Bhutanese and Nepalese Maoists. The emerging Maoist threat forced the hand of the king who was already under the pressure of India to act against these groups.

The Bhutanese action initiated the process of cooperation in counter-terrorism in South Asia. The risk taken by Bhutan to uproot the terrorists from its territory has only increased the significance of its action. While the military action was on, countries like Bangladesh sealed their borders with India to prevent the insurgents fleeing Bhutan or Myanmar from entering its territory. It also took sporadic action against insurgents operating from its territory. There were indications that Myanmar was also tightening the noose on Indian insurgent groups like the NSCN-K and the ULFA, which has bases in the country.

## The Clean-up in Bangladesh

The insurgent groups active in Northeast India always have been tempted to take shelter in Bangladesh and operate from there as that part of India is locked by Bangladesh. As a result almost all Northeast insurgent groups had camps in Bangladesh. The situation became worse after the emergence of religious extremist groups in Bangladesh. Though these groups primarily posed a threat to Bangladesh, India also was affected. Their links with Pak based groups enhanced this threat. This nexus also provided Pakistani groups an alternative route for entering India.

The presence of Indian Insurgent Groups (IIGs) in Bangladesh has often made the law and order situation, volatile in that country. The IIGs that have in the past used Bangladeshi territory for terror operations against India have on many occasions indulged in fratricidal killings. They were also suspected of having a role in some of the political attacks that have taken place in Bangladesh which has had a serious impact on the law and order situation in the country. This has made Bangladesh an important transit route for arms trafficking. Cox's Bazaar in Bangladesh has emerged as a major hub for supply of illegal arms and ammunition to northeast insurgents.[4]

The biggest consignment of smuggled arms was seized on April 2, 2004 when the Bangladesh police and coastguard raided the government-controlled Chittagong Urea Fertiliser Limited (CUFL). Reports indicated that, in this seizure, the smugglers were unloading the weapons with help from local police.

The Awami League after coming to power has restarted investigation of the Chittagong arms seizure. It has unmasked the government officials and agencies involved in arms trafficking. The investigation has now also conclusively proved that the arms were meant for Northeast insurgents.[5] The arrested smugglers have revealed that senior political leaders along with civil and military intelligence chiefs of then four-party alliance government were involved in the botched arms shipment.[6] The Sheikh Hasina government prosecuted two former Bangladesh army generals, Major General Rezakul Haider Chowdhury and Brigadier General Abdur Rahim, who headed the National Security Intelligence (NSI).[7] They were prosecuted for facilitating the landing of Chinese arms meant for insurgents in India's Northeast and for trying to smuggle these arms into India. It is also reported that Paresh Barua himself supervised the unloading of arms. Clearly, Bangladesh had to play a very important role if terrorism in south Asia was to be checked.

When Sheikh Hasina came to power for the first time, she disbanded most of the "overground" training camps of these insurgents. It was during the Awami

League's regime that the ULFA leader Anup Chetia was arrested, convicted and jailed, while there were up to four attempts on the life Paresh Barua the leader of the group's armed wing. This forced Paresh Barua to leave Dhaka and move to Karachi. Though Karachi was safe, it was too far off and it was difficult to run a rebellion in Assam from there. Besides, the commercial interests of Barua also prompted him to return to the country. The money made from these had funded his once-powerful group.

In November 2009, the Sheikh Hasina government in Bangladesh took a significant step towards improving bilateral relations with India when it detained two top leaders of the ULFA—'foreign secretary' Sashadhar Choudhury and 'finance secretary' Chitraban Hazarika and handed them over to India.[8] Subsequently, they have also handed over ULFA chairman Arabinda Rajkhowa, his bodyguard Raja Bora and the deputy commander-in-chief Raju Barua. This has provided a much needed impetus to counter-terror cooperation in South Asia. Recently, Bangladesh has also handed over Ranjan Daimary of the pro-sovereignty faction of the National Democratic Front of Bodoland (NDFB). A series of crackdowns on camps of Indian insurgents has forced them to cross over and surrender to Indian authorities. The cooperation of Bangladesh has dealt a major blow to insurgency and terrorism in the Northeast.

Bangladesh has also acted against the religious extremist groups active domestically such as the HUJI and the JMB. It has busted several local modules of LeT and Jaish-e-Mohammad. This crackdown has averted several attacks within Bangladesh and resulted in a setback to the terror network inside the country. It has shared information with India on the basis of which arrests have been made in India as well.

## Myanmar

Myanmar has been another favourite base for Indian insurgents for three important reasons. The insurgents used this country as a safe base after East Pakistan (Bangladesh) became unavailable to them immediately after its liberation. Myanmar is also used as crucial link zone through which rebels could go to China for training and weapons. It also provides a safe training and regrouping zone where new recruits can be taught guerrilla warfare and active guerrilla units can be shifted out to, when under pressure in India.

The policy of Myanmar towards Indian insurgent groups has been mixed. In the past, the insurgent outfits were actively supported by Myanmar as a counter to India's support for pro democracy activists in Myanmar. The IIGs crossed into Myanmar's heavily forested but porous border to be trained not only in Kachin but also in China and Thailand. The drug trade further strengthened their activities, with Myanmar's insurgent groups (like the Kachins) cooperating with Indian insurgent groups like ULFA and NSCN.

These groups have also allowed the setting up of training camps for terrorist outfits like ULFA. This support can be attributed to the fact that such groups on both sides have been fighting against the state and more importantly ethnic affinity has deepened the collaboration in case of Nagas. The Naga tribes are present on both the sides of the border and therefore they found it easier to operate from Myanmar with the help of their brethren. The Naga rebels set up a powerful base in Somra Hills facing Manipur. Sinkaling Hkamti and Noklak served as the headquarters of the Naga Federal Army in the 1960s and 1970s.[9]

Although during the 1990s the Tatmadaw (Myanmar military) signed about 17 major ceasefire agreements with rebel groups, two dozen armed opposition groups are still active in pockets around Myanmar's remote border regions, including the Karen National Union, the Shan State Army (South) and the Karen National Liberation Army. Such armed groups have made common cause with insurgents in India and they collectively set up the Indo-Burma Revolutionary Front in May 1990. The aim was to create a vast network for financial and ammunition exchanges. Although it soon disintegrated due to internal disputes, it had brought together major insurgent groups like Kachin Independent Army (KIA), National Socialist Council of Nagaland-Isak Muivah (ISCN-IM), United Liberation Front of Asom (ULFA), United National Liberation Front-Manipur (UNLF-M), and the People's Liberation Army (PLA) from both sides of the border.[10]

Following improvement in relations, India and Myanmar conducted joint military operations—'Operation Goldenbird' (May 1995) and 'Operation Leech' (1996). In the 'Operation Goldenbird' the Indian and Myanmarese armies launched a pincer attack on a group of some 200 Indian insurgents along the border with Mizoram. Up to 60 ULFA and other Northeast Indian insurgents were killed and several others arrested during the 44-day offensive. The insurgents were returning to their bases in India after procuring a huge consignment of arms from Bangladesh. This military co-operation has been generally continuing between the two nations despite some ups and downs in recent years.

In the year 2000, ULFA signed an agreement for joint operations with the UNLF. The ULFA described it as a 'fraternal bond sealed to fulfil certain tactical goals.' But actually this agreement was reached as ULFA, under pressure in Bhutan, was scouting for new safe havens and was eyeing UNLF's bases and training facilities in Myanmar and Bangladesh. As UNLF had an excellent equations with the junta in Myanmar the ULFA apparently wanted to take advantage of this.

Myanmar has not decisively turned against IIGs. In December 2001, as many as 192 UNLF cadres, including some top leaders, were 'arrested' by the Myanmarese army. All of them were set free by February 14, 2002, in four phases. At the same time the regime in Yangon kept promising Indian leaders support in checking cross-border insurgency. Similarly, the Meitei rebels of Manipur captured inside Myanmar were set free instead of being handed over to Indian authorities.

Myanmar's stand towards the Northeastern insurgents is ambiguous. Their army has been selectively targeting Indian rebels. As a result, despite occasional crackdowns on the NSCN Khaplang, the ULFA and PLA, rebels have been functioning from there without any problems. According to Indian militants, no government would be able to dismantle all NSCN camps or ULFA bases in Myanmar, as some of the Tatmadaw officers have very close ties with the leaders of these groups, who have been using the Sagaing division as a launch pad for their trafficking and terrorist activities. It has been reported that after fleeing from Bangladesh in 2008, ULFA's 28 battalion and a group of KLO rebels took shelter in Myanmar (Sagning, Lunglang, and Huweit) under the protection of NSCN (K).

## Counter-terror Cooperation with Sri Lanka

Sri Lanka has been facing problem from the LTTE which had initially been formed to get a due share for the Tamil population from the Sri Lankan state. Gradually however spreading terror became its predominant objective. Its supremo Prabhakaran in his later years was no longer keen to reach a negotiated solution with the Sri Lankan state.

Sri Lanka has now managed to overpower the LTTE threat and the state seems to be contemplating various formulae to accommodate Tamil interests. To fight the LTTE threat Sri Lankan state received military hardware from various countries including China, Pakistan and Israel. It was difficult for India to help the Sri Lankan state with military hardware keeping in view the sensitivities of the large Tamil population in India. But India did contribute to the Sri Lankan effort by sending non-lethal equipment like radars. It also shared vital intelligence with Sri Lankan military that made a real difference. On the basis of these inputs various ships carrying armaments for the LTTE were destroyed which weakened the LTTE and led to its elimination.

## Counter-terror Cooperation with Maldives

The Indian Ocean archipelago of the Maldives does not share a land boundary with any of the South Asian nations. But it does share the Indian Ocean with some of these countries. The Maldives does not pose any direct threat to Indian security, but there is a growing radicalisation in the country where multi-party democracy has been recently introduced. The government of President Nasheed is aware of the problem and is working seriously to counter the threat.

Several Maldivians have been killed in fighting along with Al-Qaeda cadres in Waziristan and NWFP. Some of them also have been arrested. Maldivians are also being educated in Indian and Pakistani madrassas. President Nasheed's government is concerned about this phenomenon. Nasheed recently pointed out that the Indian Ocean is the soft underbelly of India as seen in the 26/11 terror attack. It is heartening to note that India and the Maldives have decided to cooperate. Indian ships have been permitted to patrol waters close to Maldives.

There is also fear in some quarters that the LeT might try to establish base in Maldives as many of its islands are still not inhabited. But President Nasheed has been emphatic in saying that there is no LeT presence in Maldives.

## Nepal

Maoists in Nepal who were earlier fighting the state have decided to join democratic politics. This is an interesting experiment. It would be the first case of the successful mainstreaming of a rebel group which is quite big and has a significant influence in the country's population.

It would also have implications for India, where large parts have been affected by similar rebellion. The world today is clueless about mainstreaming Taliban. The successful mainstreaming of Maoists in Nepal might give some clue.

## Pakistan and Afghanistan

The situation in Pakistan and Afghanistan requires a combined analyses as the Taliban's sway over both countries increases. For successful counter-terror cooperation in South Asia, it is imperative that India and Pakistan also cooperate. Unfortunately, this cooperation is not as forthcoming as has been the case between India and other countries. The denial of terror emanating from Pakistan is passé.

Pakistan presently seems to be going through a churning process. A weak democratic government is pitted against a traditionally strong army, which has its own world view. In recent times, Islamist groups like Tahriq-e-Taliban have also become important players. Thus a three cornered struggle for dominance appears to be underway in Pakistan. The country is a state of flux, which has not given these players enough time for a major rethink of existing policies. On the other hand, the objective of gaining strategic depth by having greater say over the affairs of Afghanistan has further muddled the whole situation.

A clear Pakistani approach towards counter-terrorism is not likely to emerge till a strong democratic government takes root in the country and realises like the government in Bangladesh that terrorists are not its friends. The situation in Afghanistan and Pakistan has emerged as a big headache not only for South Asia but also for the rest of the world. This is why major Western powers also in Afghanistan under ISAF and NATO. Unfortunately, they also do not seem to be getting a grip on the problem and the worsening crisis in the West has made them look for quickest exit route.

## Cooperation under SAARC

The SAARC Regional Convention on Suppression of Terrorism which was signed on November 4, 1987 came into force on August 22, 1988 following its ratification by all member states. But cooperation under the banner of SAARC has not been successful for precisely the reasons mentioned above.

At the 11th summit in Kathmandu in January 2002, SAARC leaders once again took a pledge to make collective efforts to stamp out terrorism. At the Islamabad summit in January 2004, the member countries adopted the additional protocol to the SAARC's Regional Convention on Suppression of Terrorism. During the Dhaka summit, the additional protocol to the SAARC's Regional Convention on Suppression of Terrorism came into effect with all the seven member countries ratifying it to "wage a joint war against terrorism".

Though all member countries ratified the protocol, it will require some changes to be made in the Criminal Procedure Code (CrPC) of the respective countries so that it can be implemented. The member states will have to formulate necessary laws to implement the protocol on terrorism. But most importantly, the effectiveness of this agreement would depend on the sincerity with which it is implemented. If implemented, the protocol would also enable them to take measures to prevent and suppress the financing of terrorist activities.

Some progress was also achieved during the Colombo SAARC summit where leaders of South Asian countries reached an agreement to put in place a regional legal framework to tackle the scourge. The SAARC Convention on Mutual Legal Assistance in Criminal Matters is expected to strengthen regional cooperation in the fight against cross-border crimes, in particular the fight against terrorism. In this respect, the Convention calls on all state parties to provide each other the widest possible cooperation for combating crime by strengthening cooperation in the prevention, investigation and prosecution of crimes. The support extended is subject to the national laws of the state parties to the Convention. The Convention outlines the procedure to be followed in investigations, including search and seizure, obtaining evidence, documents and witnesses in the provision of mutual legal assistance.

The Sheikh Hasina government after taking over also talked of setting up a regional task force for countering terrorism. But the government soon very wisely realised that it was much better for the countries to act individually against terror than to wait for regional cooperation to take off.

## Conclusion

South Asia has made major progress in counter-terror cooperation. Now terror groups in most South Asian countries are not seen as assets. On the other hand, most of these countries have realised that presence of such groups within their territories makes the security situation volatile and poses a threat to them. This has prompted action against several terrorist and insurgent groups. As desire to eliminate these forces has emerged, many countries are refusing to see insurgents as freedom fighters, leading to clear-cut action against them. This has dramatically changed the security situation in a large part of South Asia. This opportunity if properly utilised may lead to an economic boom in many of these countries. Sri Lanka, Bangladesh and Bhutan seem to be the major beneficiaries of this.

The countries which are hamstrung are those who have not been decisive in their approach towards terrorism.

In Nepal, though the Maoists have given up arms the country has failed to evolve an alternative functioning democratic system. It y is constrained by inability of both sides to come to a common ground and write a constitution for democratic Nepal.

Pakistan and Afghanistan seem to be internally in major turmoil. The continued crisis has often raised questions about their survival. Though these countries have managed to keep their geographical territory intact, the development process seems to have suffered, giving further opportunity to extremist and terrorist forces. A strong SAARC could have attempted to solve the crisis in Af-Pak region. But as SAARC itself struggles it has given allowed external powers to come in and make attempts to control the situation.

If the countries of the region have a genuine desire to cooperate on counter-terrorism then this cooperation should not be kept hostage to legal regimes. In any case, the interpretation of the law depends on people who are supposed to follow it. So even if some agreement is reached and the member countries are not willing to cooperate then they would achieve little. On the other hand, if the countries are sincere about fighting terrorism then they would find ways to cooperate as has been shown by Bangladesh. South Asia has to decide whether it wants to overpower terror or will it allow terror to overpower it.

## Notes

1. Anand Kumar, "Bhutan's Offensive against the Terrorists" Institute of Peace and Conflict Studies, Article # 1258, 28 December 2003, at http://ipcs.org/article/bhutan/bhutans-offensive-against-the-terrorists-1258.html
2. Ibid,
3. Wasbir Hussain, "Insurgency in India's Northeast Cross-border Links and Strategic Alliances," *Faultlines,* Volume 17, New Delhi, at http://www.satp.org/satporgtp/publication/faultlines/volume17/wasbir.htm
4. Saswati Chanda and Alok Kumar Gupta, "Pakistan-Bangladesh Nexus in Abetting Insurgency in India's Northeast," in Dipankar Sengupta and Sudhir Kumar Singh edited "*Insurgency in North-East India: The Role of Bangladesh,"* Authors Press, New Delhi, 2004, p. 279.
5. "Arms found in Bangladesh meant for Indian insurgent group," IANS, June 9th, 2009 at http://www.thaindian.com/newsportal/world-news/arms-found-in-bangladesh-meant-for-indian-insurgent-group_100202554.html
6. Zia government behind botched ULFA arms shipment, court told, IANS, 5 March 2009 at http://www.thaindian.com/newsportal/world-news/zia-government-behind-botched-ulfa-arms-shipment-court-told_100162786.html
7. Dhaka to prosecute 2 former spy chiefs smuggling arms for Indian rebels, IANS, 18 May, 2009 at http://www.thaindian.com/newsportal/world-news/dhaka-to-prosecute-2-former-spy-chiefs-smuggling-arms-for-indian-rebels_100194036.html
8. Border Security Force arrest two ULFA leaders along India-Bangladesh border, *The Times of India*, 7 November 2009 at http://timesofindia.indiatimes.com/india/Border-Security-Force-arrest-two-ULFA-leaders-along-India-Bangladesh-border/articleshow/5204738.cms, also see "Assam unveils Ulfa leaders caught in Bangladesh," The Telegraph (Kolkata), November 8, 2009, at http://www.telegraphindia.com/1091108/jsp/nation/story_11714009.jsp#
9. Pradip Saikia, "Northeast India as a Factor in India's Diplomatic Engagement with Myanmar: Issues and Challenges," *Strategic Analysis*, New Delhi, Vol. 33, No 6, November 2009, pp. 880-881.
10. Pradip Saikia, p. 881.

# 12

# *Counter-terrorism and Regional Cooperation in South Asia*

*Chiran Jung Thapa*

## Background

South Asia has been a region riddled by innumerable manifestations of political violence. But, in the absence of a clearly defined or even regionally accepted definition, making a distinction between terrorism and various forms of political violence is a challenge. This has been further compounded by visceral inter-state rivalries—mainly between India and Pakistan. And despite being critically plagued by the scourge of terrorism, all efforts to develop a robust regional mechanism to respond to the challenges posed by the terrorism have yielded very little.

South Asia can be termed as the epicentre of terrorism. Today, with the increasing numbers of suicide bombings, this tactic has become almost synonymous with terrorism. Although this tactic was used in Lebanon, it was the LTTE that perfected this tactic, employed it with lethality and inspired other terrorist groups to use it elsewhere. Another salient fact about terrorism in South Asia is that three heads of states in the region have succumbed to terrorist attacks. Rajiv Gandhi was killed by an LTTE suicide bomber in 1991; followed in 1993 by the Sri Lankan president Ranasinghe Premadasa who was also assassinated by an LTTE suicide bomber, and lastly, Benazir Bhutto who was killed in a terrorist attack in 2007. Interestingly, it is also in South Asia that a terrorist organisation has been completely obliterated by brute force. Sri-Lanka has set a benchmark in counter-terrorism history by wiping out the LTTE through military operations.

There is another fact that has contributed to make this region significant in terms of terrorism. Following 9/11, South Asia has effectively taken centre stage in America's counter—'global war on terror' campaign. The Taliban regime in Afghanistan had provided a safe haven to Al-Qaeda—the terrorist outfit responsible for the attacks. The US then launched its "Operation Enduring Freedom," on October 7, 2001 to finish off the Al-Qaeda in Afghan territory. Since then, South Asia has been a major theatre for the counter-terrorism activities.

Today, nearly ten years after 9/11, South Asia has become the region hardest hit by terrorism. According to the 2009 terrorism report released by the United States' National Counter Terrorism Centre, approximately 10,999 terrorist attacks occurred in 83 countries during 2009, leaving over 58,000 injured and nearly 15,000 dead. Of the 10,999 reported attacks, about 4,850, or 44 per cent, occurred in South Asia. The three countries that had the highest number of casualties were Afghanistan, Pakistan and India. Afghanistan's casualty rate was 2,778, Pakistan's 2,670 while India had 663 deaths.

## Terrorism and Post-9/11 Scenario

The terrorist attacks on September 11, 2001, marked a turning point in the history of terrorism. The coordinated attacks (never witnessed before) demonstrated the sophistication and the ability of networked terrorist organisations like the Al-Qaeda. The magnitude of the attack was unparalleled. The economic loss and death toll was colossal. Naturally, the media coverage was expansive. The suicide mission exhibited a resolute commitment towards the cause. The fact that all of the perpetrators involved in the mission were young Muslims added another dimension. The perpetrators had deftly managed to sneak in undetected and had successfully breached the security shield of the most powerful nation on earth. This assault sent a chilling message to the rest of the world—no nation was immune or proof against the scourge of terrorism.

Following this brazen attack on its soil, the counter-terrorism strategy envisaged and later executed by the United States too ushered in a new era in global politics and gave rise to the concept of unilateralism. George Bush's strategy of pre-emption and of attacking any country that harboured terrorists was a game changer.

The United States went in and toppled governments of two sovereign countries—Iraq and Afghanistan—with brute force when it perceived that these states posed a threat to its national interest. This opened a whole new course for powerful and capable states to follow suit in the future. The message was clear—sovereignty is no longer inviolable and sacrosanct. To illustrate, the United States continues to undertake covert military missions to track and eliminate terrorists taking shelter in Pakistan. Despite strong condemnation from Pakistan, the US also continues to mount drone attacks against terrorists in its territory.

Perhaps the most important aspect of the post-9/11 scenario is that cooperation has become the hall-mark of any effective counter-terrorism strategy. During the initial stages, the United States attempted to rally support for its anti-terror actions. However, when it did not receive the support it anticipated, it bulldozed through with its agenda and took unilateral steps to wipe out terrorism. But, even with its unparalleled power, technologies and ample resources, the United States has realised that it could not fight the war on terror and the support and cooperation of other states was indispensable. Markedly, the US provides billions of dollars to Pakistan for its cooperation in its war on terror.

Along with cooperation with other states, there is an increasing realisation that cooperation between the various entities within the government was also necessary. The 9/11 commission that investigated the 9/11 attacks, highlighted the intelligence community's shortcomings arising from the lack of coordination and cooperation between the various agencies. Since then the US government has accorded high priority to cooperation and coordination between various internal agencies. In order to facilitate better cooperation between various intelligence agencies, the government created the position of a Director of National Intelligence (DNI). Likewise, the department of homeland security was also created to foster cooperation and coordination between various internal agencies.

## The "BIPA Corridor"

Statistics reveal that South Asia has been severely affected by terrorism but is mainly the corridor that extends from the Bay of Bengal to the western frontiers of Afghanistan spanning Bangladesh, India, Pakistan and Afghanistan. The corridor can be effectively termed the "BIPA corridor."

There are numerous reasons why the BIPA corridor will continue to be the hot spot for terrorist activities but primarily for the jihadi form of terrorism. The jihadi cause is of great relevance to the BIPA corridor because this region has the highest concentration of Muslims in the world. Of an estimated 1.6 billion Muslims worldwide, a little over half a billion reside in the BIPA corridor.

BIPA corridor has the greatest of potential of becoming the foremost recruiting ground for the jihadis. This is because the South Asian masses who are badly governed, mired in poverty and clobbered by natural disasters are naturally more susceptible to the lure of jihadi ideology and cause. All these elements combined together make this corridor the most potent time bomb ticking in the world today.

## Bangladesh

Bangladesh—the world's third most populous Muslim nation, has numerous Islamic militant outfits operating in its territory—its home ministry recently released a list of 12 terrorist groups active in Bangladesh. Although Bangladesh has not endured any significant terrorist attack in the last couple of years, the menace of Islamic terrorism is present under the relative tranquillity. Groups like Harkat-ul-Jehad-al Islami Bangladesh (HUJI-B), Jagrata Muslim Janata Bangladesh (JMJB), Jamaat-ul Mujahideen Bangaladesh (JMB) some groups still around in Bangladesh. There have been reports that claim that some of these banned terrorists groups are trying to re-group. There are even claims that the JMB has been trying to forge an alliance with HUJI.

The prospects of terrorism hovering over Bangladesh are illustrated by a few incidents in the recent past. Ten trucks full of modern arms and weaponry were seized by government authorities in April 2004. This was the largest arms seizure in the nation's history. Reports indicate that this amount was sufficient to arm an entire military division. On August 17, 2005, 459 time bombs were detonated in 63 districts of Bangladesh, within a matter of 40 minutes (there are 64 districts in Bangladesh). These bombs, which were about the size of salt shakers, were timed to create terror, rather cause destruction. This was a testament to the organisational capacity and reach of those that perpetrated the act. Although no one formally claimed responsibility for the attacks, the leaflets found at the blast sites mentioned the Islamic extremist group Jamaat-ul-Mujahadeen Bangladesh (JMB), and threatened judges, government officials, politicians, and other "enemies of Islam", including the United States and the United Kingdom. Through a web posting, the JMB further called for Islamic rule in Bangladesh stating that they only wanted to see the rule of Allah, and warned of further action if the Bangladeshi government tried to repress the clerics and intellectuals of Islam. Six JBM leaders including its chief—Abdur Rahman and his second-in-command Siddiqur Rahman alias Bangla Bhai were later apprehended and executed by the Bangladeshi authorities

But despite the capture of some of key terrorists, JMB activities have continued in Bangladesh. Immediately after the six JMB leaders were put on trial, a new six-member central committee took shape with Maulana Sayedur Rahman Jaffar as the acting chief of the group. A training camp operated by JMB members was raided by law enforcement agencies in September 2009. Several suspected JMB members were arrested and weapons caches that included grenades and chemicals that could be used to make explosives found.

Other jihadi outfits are also cropping up. This is illustrated by the emergence of a new group called Islam-o-Muslim (IoM)—which is believed to be a breakaway faction of the JMB. This outfit came on the government's radar following the capture of a JMB operative named Mustfizur Rahman. Later Adbur Rahim (a.k.a Shahadat Hossain) was also apprehended. The interrogation of these individuals revealed that the IoM was established by former JMB operatives in April 2009. Unlike JMB, which used various terror tactics in the country ranging from suicide attacks to planting bombs and explosives, the IoM aims to wage jihad with small arms, focusing on weapons and ammunition manufacturing in their hideouts.

The alarming aspect in Bangladesh is the host of factors that are conducive for the spread of terrorism. Factors such as high youth unemployment, acute economic disparity, rising religious fervour, and easy availability of firearms serve to fuel terrorist activities. Bangladesh's unguarded sea frontier can also be used by terrorists to enter without difficulty. The fact that Bangladeshi terrorist outfits have linkages with other terror outfits in the region only makes matters worse. On July 2009, Bangladesh police arrested a Lashkar-e-Tayyeba (LeT) operative, Mufti Obaidullah (a.k.a Abu Zafa). Obaidullah, originally from India, reportedly told his interrogators that his task was to organise jihad in Bangladesh in cooperation with HuJi and JMB operatives. He further revealed that the Pakistan based LeT has been active in Bangladesh for the last 14 years. He also said that Bangladeshi outfits have been linked to the network of the absconding Indian mafia don Dawood Ibrahim, and also to leaders of other Islamist militant organisations.

## India

India has been afflicted by terrorism, secessionist movements and other low-intensity conflicts for long. India continues to face protracted insurgencies in the Northeastern states of Arunachal Pradesh, Assam, Manipur, Meghalaya, Mizoram, Nagaland and Tripura. Jammu and Kashmir (J&K) in north western India still remains its most volatile region. Historically, this state has been the victim of the largest number of terrorist attacks. India has persistently blamed Pakistan for providing support to militant outfits operating in this region. On the other hand, there is a long history of Maoist left-wing extremists also known as Naxals operating in large swathes of central and eastern India. Lately, the

Maoists have escalated their activities and attacks. According to India's home minister, Maoists are wreaking havoc in 223 districts across 20 states, out of a total of 636 districts in 28 states. The Maoist/Naxals, are mainly active in the states of Andhra Pradesh, Bihar, Chhattisgarh, Jharkhand, Karnataka, Orissa, and West Bengal. These states are collectively referred to as the "Red Corridor." Given the surge of Maoist activities, the Indian prime minister has even told parliament that this represents the most significant threat to domestic security. Then, there are other Islamic radical groups with transnational links. Groups such as Student Islamic Movement of India (SIMI), LeT, Harkat-ul-Mujhahideen, Jaish-e-Mohammad, and Harkar-ul-Ansar are still operational and pose a significant threat. Today, there are 34 outfits designated as terrorist by the government of India.

Over the last decade, there have been numerous large scale and small scale attacks in India. In 2001, J&K legislative assembly was attacked. That same year, there was another brazen terrorist attack on the Indian Parliament. In 2003 too, there were a number of quite a few terrorist attacks. Then, in 2005, the capital city was jolted by another major attack. Three bombs exploded and killed 62 people and wounded another 200 or so.

The terrorist incidents in India that got global attention in recent times have mostly occurred in Mumbai. In July 2006, a series of bombs were detonated by terrorists on local train network in Mumbai. The seven bombs that were set off within 11 minutes took 209 lives and injured another 700. Then, there was a series of coordinated attacks on November 26 2008. Commonly referred to as "26/11", terrorists struck at several locations including two hotels, a Jewish centre, the main train station, and killed at least 183 people including 22 foreigners. Over 300 others were injured. The attackers had also planted bombs in two taxis which later exploded in different locations in the city.

Most of the terrorist attacks on India have been carried out by Islamic terrorists with linkages in Pakistan. These trans-border terrorist groups not only have the potential to inflict significant damage but they can also serve to escalate tensions between India and Pakistan. Since India and Pakistan have gone to war several times in the past, the likelihood of war due to terrorist activities is a real possibility. To illustrate, after the capture of Ajmal Kasab, the only surviving terrorist of the Mumbai terrorist attacks, investigations revealed that the ten armed attackers were Pakistani nationals and were trained and sent by the LeT—a Pakistani based terrorist outfit. When this fact was exposed, the India was naturally seething. Pakistan initially denied that Pakistanis were responsible for the attacks and instead blamed plotters in Bangladesh and Indian criminals. While the relations between these two countries soured further, there were murmurs of another Indo-Pak conflict. Later, however, Pakistan acknowledged that the terrorists involved were Pakistanis and a bitter tussle between these two mortal enemies was averted.

Another salient aspect regarding terrorism in India is its Muslim population. There are about 170 million Muslims in India. This is noteworthy because of the religious divide between the Hindus and Muslims in India. India has witnessed numerous sectarian clashes in the past. Further unrest stemming from the religious divide between these two groups is still a great possibility. Second, the Muslim population in India is another great resource for the Islamic terrorists both for providing a safe haven and for moral support. Third, following any terrorist attack on India perpetrated by Islamic terror groups, security forces naturally target the Muslim communities. Since Muslims become the victims of witch-hunts during the investigation process, it creates a sense of alienation. And the terrorist groups exploit the alienation factor to their advantage.

Although there have been no large-scale terrorist assaults similar to the 2008 attacks in Mumbai, experts have continually warned that India still remains at risk. Should the recent attack be mentioned? The Indian Home Minister has claimed that dozens of terrorist attempts have been foiled by intelligence and law enforcement agencies. And most recently, he has further warned against the rise of "Saffron terrorism". The investigations into the Malegaon, Mecca Masjid and Ajmer Sharif attacks have pointed to the involvement of Hindu radical groups. In a country where most terrorist activities are perpetrated by Islamic outfits, the revelation of Hindu affiliated terrorism has rung new alarm bells.

## Pakistan

Pakistan has been dubbed as the most dangerous country on the planet for obvious reasons. Pakistan is a nuclear weapon state beset by underdevelopment, poor socio-economic conditions, rising population and growing unemployment. This has been exacerbated by lack of robust governance. Pakistan has regularly oscillated between military rule and civilian rule. A fragile polity established and home to South Asia's Muslim population still suffers tremendously from sectarian rifts. Pakistan has also become the epicentre of Islamist extremism. Foreign terrorist organisations including Al-Qaeda and its affiliates continue to operate and carry out attacks in Pakistan. If this were not bad enough, it was recently hit by one of the worst natural calamities in human history when it was inundated by floods in July 2010. An estimated 200,000 died, a million homes were destroyed and about 20 million affected by the unprecedented floods.

Pakistan has continued to suffer from rising militancy and extremism for a number of years. Since the US toppled the Taliban regime in 2001, Al-Qaeda and Taliban remnants are believed to have shifted their bases to the Federally

Administered Tribal Areas (FATA) of Pakistan have found safe havens in Pakistani cities such as Quetta and Peshawar, as well as in the rugged Pakistan-Afghanistan border region. And Al-Qaeda is reportedly making alliances with indigenous Pakistani terrorist groups.

The former US Director of National Intelligence, John Negroponte's remarks on Pakistan encapsulate its role in the "war on terror." According to him, Pakistan is a frontline partner in the war on terror. But, he alleged, that it still remains a major source of Islamic extremism and is home to some of the top terrorist leaders in the world. Cross-border infiltration of Islamist militants supported by Pakistan who cross the Kashmir Line of Control (LOC) to engage in terrorist acts against India are also a significant threat to the relations between these two countries and to the stability of the region.

Domestic terrorism in Pakistan, much of it associated with Islamist sectarianism, has become a serious problem affecting many Pakistani cities. Terrorist acts stemming from Sunni-Shia sectarian strife and ethnic tensions have become a major concern in Pakistan. Attacks targeting the country's major urban centres, including Peshawar, Karachi, Lahore, Islamabad, and Rawalpindi, are on the rise. The number of suicide bombings too has surged and have often resulted in large numbers of casualties, with about 50 per cent of them occurring in Islamabad, Lahore, Peshawar, and Rawalpindi.

Terrorist attacks in Pakistan demonstrate the sheer ability of these terrorists. They have mounted coordinated and complex attacks and chosen high-value targets, and struck with great precision. There have been brazen attacks on key security targets in retaliation for Pakistani military operations in Swat and throughout FATA. Besides targeting security forces, government institutions and elected representatives, terrorists have systematically targeted perceived adversaries, such as aid workers, religious scholars, journalists, diplomats, senior military officers, and educational institutions.

The most alarming aspect about terrorism in Pakistan, however, is the involvement of the state. There are doubts in many quarters about the determination, sincerity, and effectiveness of the Pakistani government's effort to combat terrorism. India constantly harps about Pakistan's involvement in terrorism. It alleges that Pakistan has aided terrorists groups that perpetrate acts of terror in Indian territory and beyond. Although the US considers Pakistan a key ally in the war on terror, many top US officials still suspect that Pakistan is maintaining linkages with militants and terrorist groups. Pakistan through its intelligence agency—ISI is often accused of harbouring world's most dangerous terrorist groups like Al-Qaeda, Lashkar-e-Omar, LeT, Sipah-e-Sahaba, Jaish-e-Mohammad, Harkat-ul-Mujahideen, and Hizbul Mujahideen.

Another major concern in Pakistan is terrorist financing. Many illegal, unlicenced informal "hawala" (money changers) are still operational in many parts of Pakistan. The informal and secretive nature of these hawala transactions makes it very difficult to trace the origin and recipients of illicit funds.

## Afghanistan

Since the 9/11 terrorist attacks, Afghanistan has remained in the limelight for counter-terrorism activities. Primarily, the perpetrators of the 9/11 attacks had been sheltered and trained in Afghanistan. The Taliban regime had provided Al-Qaeda a safe haven in Afghan territory. It was in Afghanistan where the US lead counter-terrorism campaign began. And even today the Taliban and Al-Qaeda make their presence felt through intermittent acts of terrorism.

There are still some lethal outfits that continue to remain as major threats in Afghanistan. The significant ones are Al-Qaeda, the Taliban, the Haqquani network and the Hizb-e-Islami (HeI). Although their influence and operational capabilities might have diminished due to the counter-terrorism activities launched by the Afghan government with the assistance of allied troops, these groups still have the capability to mount some devastating attacks. All three groups are not only active in the Afghan territory but also across the border in Pakistan. Many reckon that the Taliban and Al-Qaeda have maintained an operational relationship.

Since the West toppled the Taliban regime, this country has effectively become a battleground between the allied forces stationed there and various Islamic militants. Islamic militants from all over the world are reported to be operating in Afghanistan. Since many view the stationing of foreign troops in Afghanistan as the Christian occupation of Islamic territory, many have come to assist their Muslim brothers engaged in a holy war against the West.

Another salient aspect is the narcotics production and export business in Afghanistan. Many apply the term "narco-terrorism" to Afghanistan. Afghanistan is ranked as the number one illicit opium producer and exporter in the world. Opium production in Afghanistan has risen since the downfall of the Taliban in 2001. Above 90 per cent of the opiates in the world market are believed to originate in Afghanistan. Afghanistan is also the world's largest producer of hashish. The billions of dollars raked from export of such narcotic substances are believed to be pocketed by insurgents, warlords, drug traffickers and terrorist groups. Hence, many believe that narcotics export is fuelling terrorism in the country.

Another worrying aspect about Afghanistan is the dismal level of development in the country. Despite the billions of dollars poured into Afghanistan by various donors, the country's overall development is still unsatisfactory. It is still one of the poorest countries in the world. The United Nations Development Programme's (UNDP) Human Development Report of 2009 ranks Afghanistan at the very bottom. It has been ranked 181 out of 182 countries. Even the Human Poverty Index (HPI) ranks Afghanistan at the very bottom of 135 countries in terms of human deprivation, characterised by short life, lack of basic education, and lack of access to public and private resources. As pointed out earlier, impoverishment and under-development are some of the root factors that have been identified as the catalysts of terrorism. From these afore-mentioned facts, one can easily understand why the prospects of terrorism in Afghanistan remain so high.

## SAARC, Regional Cooperation and Counter-terrorism

Since the birth of SAARC in 1985, the member states have collectively acknowledged that terrorism is a danger to society. Although the intent behind the establishment of SAARC was the promotion of regional cooperation for economic development and trade issues, countering terrorism through regional cooperation has been high on the agenda from its early years. During the first summit held in Dhaka in 1985, the heads of state of the SAARC had duly recognised the dangers posed by the spread of terrorism and its harmful impact on peace, cooperation, friendship and good neighbourly relations. They were also aware that terrorism could also jeopardise the sovereignty and territorial integrity of states. Hence in 1987, only two years after its formation, SAARC approved the Regional Convention on Suppression of Terrorism. An additional Protocol to this convention was signed at the Islamabad summit in 2004. Also, during the summit, the heads of states gave their support to the UNSC resolution 1373 and made commitments to suppress terrorism in all its forms and manifestations.

The Regional Convention on Suppression of Terrorism and Additional Protocol on Terrorism constitutes a single document under which the member countries have pledged to initiate, within their national legal frameworks, certain measures to combat terrorism by suppressing and eradicating the financing of terrorism, seizing and confiscating of funds and other assets, preventing money laundering, cooperation on immigration and customs control, cooperation among law enforcement agencies, providing mutual legal assistance and holding consultations among them. Furthermore, at the 15th summit held in Colombo in 2008, member states accorded terrorism number one priority and pledged to fight terrorism collectively.

Other mechanisms have also been set up for counter-terrorism activities. A SAARC Terrorism Monitoring Desk (STOMD) has been established in Colombo since 1995 to "collate, analyse and disseminate information about terrorist incidents, tactics, strategies and methods." On February 2009, during a SAARC council of ministers' meeting a declaration on "Cooperation and Combating terrorism" was made. Pakistan recently hosted SAARC interior ministers' conference in Islamabad in July 2010. The agenda of the conference included the discussions on preparing a common counter-terrorism strategy, cooperation in police matters and information sharing mechanisms, preventing human trafficking, visa issues, law-enforcement, curbing smuggling of narcotics, drugs and psychotropic substances.

Leaders of SAARC member states have accorded counter-terrorism the number one priority in SAARC and numerous pledges and commitments have been made to collectively combat it and eventually eliminate it. However, commitments and pledges have remained confined to pronouncements and no tangible headway has been made to collectively work against terrorism. Essentially, the regional mechanism has been hobbled by inter-state tensions, mutual mistrust, suspicion and reluctance to implement the adopted agreements.

There are two main hurdles that impede a functioning regional counter-terrorism strategy. First, there is a definition discrepancy and double standards. Second, the India-Pakistan rivalry has stymied any regional initiatives on countering terrorism.

## Definition Discrepancy and Double Standards

Back in 2003, while addressing the members of Bundestag, the German parliament, Indian Prime Minister Atal Bihari Vajpayee decried the "double standards" adopted by countries in combating terrorism and alleged that India had suffered from both terrorism and from the consequences of the double standards applied by countries to deal with terrorism. He was apparently referring to how the West, particularly the American approach and interpretations of the cross-border terrorism in Jammu and Kashmir. He felt that Jammu and Kashmir was a genuine case of terrorism but the US did not view it as such and was not applying enough pressure on Pakistan. India regards Pakistan as a catalyst of violence in J&K.

The above reflects two issues. First, there is a distinct discrepancy in the definition. Even today, a universally accepted definition of "terrorism" is sorely lacking. Even amongst the member states of the UN, there is still no consensus on this issue. Currently, in the absence of a universally endorsed definition of terrorism, countries continue to make their own interpretations and employ their own local laws and judicial and administrative pronouncements as they see fit. Second, there are clear double standards when it comes to dealing with terrorists and terrorism. The aphorism that "one man's terrorist is another man's freedom fighter" is still very prevalent.

There are ample examples of countries that cry foul over "double standards" but engage in dubious activities themselves. In 2008, Sri Lanka's state-run *Sunday Observer* had published an interview with the country's army chief, Sarath Fonseka. In the interview, General Fonseka had lambasted some Indian politicians for supporting the LTTE—India had banned LTTE as a terrorist outfit since 1992. Nepal's Maoists are another case in point. Although the Maoists were branded as terrorists and had red corner Interpol notices out for their arrest, India played a prominent role in facilitating the alliance of the Maoists with the other Nepali political parties through a 12 point agreement signed between the two sides in Delhi. Essentially, India orchestrated a shotgun wedding of between a banned Nepali terrorist group and the democratic forces of Nepal to emasculate the unheeding Nepali monarch.

However, the case of Pakistan's double standards is even more apparent. Although Pakistan claims to be a victim of terrorism, in July 2009, Pakistani President Asif Ali Zardari admitted that the Pakistani government had set up and nurtured terrorist groups to achieve its short-term foreign policy goals. According to a 2008 analysis published by Saban Center for Middle East Policy at Brookings Institution, Pakistan was regarded as the world's most active state sponsor of terrorism. Pakistan thorough its intelligence agency—ISI, has been frequently accused of providing support to nefarious terrorist groups and abetting these groups in perpetrating acts of terror.

## Indo-Pak Rivalry

During the 2006 non-aligned meeting held in Havana, Pakistan's president Pervez Musharraf and Indian Prime Minister ManMohan Singh had pledged to set up a bilateral Joint Anti-Terrorism Mechanism (JATM). The objective of this institutional mechanism was collaboration between India and Pakistan for identifying and implementing counter-terrorism initiatives and investigations. This had marked a new beginning to tackle terrorism as a collective threat. Despite recognising and acknowledging the threat posed by terrorism, and despite the repeated pledges made by the top leaders of these two countries to cooperate in tackling the scourge of terrorism, the mechanism has failed to make any significant progress. This initiative has not moved beyond limited information sharing. In fact, there is still a huge trust deficit between these two countries. And the bone of contention that has forestalled the momentum is Kashmir.

As has been clearly evident, the India-Pakistan rivalry is mainly to blame for the stagnant regional response towards terrorism. The conflict that began with the birth of these two nations in 1947 has been punctuated by bouts of outright wars and covert wars. Any semblance of cooperation on dealing with terrorism is difficult to even envision because the level of distrust between these two runs deep. The fact that each often accuses the other of harbouring terrorists and fomenting terrorist activities in each other's territories has only complicated things further. The case of Pakistani prime minister Yusuf Raza Gilani, avoiding Indian air space skies en route to participate in the Thimpu SAARC summit of 2010 speaks volumes about the relationship between Pakistan and India. He flew to Bhutan via Nepal, using Chinese territory in Tibet rather than taking the straightforward route through India. The prospect of cooperation on a sensitive issue such as combating terrorism can be easily discerned from this recent example.

## Recommendations

- ***Develop a consensual definition of terrorism:*** In the absence of a clearly defined and accepted classification of terrorists and terrorism, a viable regional counter-terrorism strategy is unlikely to be effective. Only when it is clearly defined can befitting measures be envisaged. And that is not sufficient. It has to be further accepted and endorsed by the members of the region. Only then can the implementation process begin.
- ***Eliminate double standards:*** Double standards inhibit the regional response capacity. If regional members merely offer lip service, it renders the task of countering terrorism even more arduous. Members have to be on the same page to be able to tackle the problem together. One country's terrorist must be another country's terrorist and nothing else.
- ***Upgrade the SAARC Terrorism Monitoring Desk into a regional Counter-Terrorism Centre.*** This centre could collect and disseminate regional data for all terrorism related activities. Since sharing of certain information between member states is still a prickly issue, this centre could potentially serve as an open source data bank. It could also become a hub for scholars and other intellectuals working on terrorism related issues. Various research activities and studies on understanding terrorism could be undertaken at this centre.
- ***Capacity building of law enforcement agencies***: One step that all SAARC members can unilaterally take is the upgrading their respective law-enforcement agencies. One of the effective counter-terrorism strategies is having robust government institutions in place. Hence, capacity building of law enforcement agencies could certainly augment the counter-terrorism initiatives. This initiative mainly requires the willingness and commitment of respective governments.

- ***Explore people-centric counter-terrorism strategies:*** Most of the counter-terrorism strategies are state-centric that rely heavily on the use of force. They focus on enhancing the state's ability to take countervailing measures against terrorist threats. For a counter-terrorism strategy to be effective, it should incorporate an element of human security. When the state and its people come together and act in unison for a common purpose, the prospects of an effective strategy become brighter. Therefore, engagement with civil society and media as a part of the campaign would greatly benefit society as a whole.
- ***Collectively work on indisputable agendas first:*** It is evident that there are great differences between member states in SAARC over various issues pertaining to terrorism. However, there are plenty of issues of common interest such as proliferation of small arms, smuggling of illicit narcotic substances, illicit money laundering and organised crime inherently linked with terrorism on which they can make common cause.

## Conclusion

Modern day terrorism has a complex and multidimensional character. It transcends borders. And the recent coordinated terrorist attacks demonstrate that modern day terrorists have developed the dexterity and sophistication to plan, train and execute acts of terror with lethality and precision.

And although South Asia continues to be plagued by the rising wave of terrorism, the countries in the region still have not been able to collectively deal with this menace. More so, SAARC—an existing regional cooperation mechanism has abysmally failed to evolve as an effective regional mechanism to deal with the most severe challenge to the region. Although, there are arrangements/ structures within SAARC to deal with terrorism, the failure can be directly attributed to the reluctance of member states to genuinely embrace and implement the agreements. Until the member states of SAARC, particularly India and Pakistan see tangible benefits in taking on terrorism any regional counter measure will turn out to be a dud just like JATM.

Hence, what South Asia sorely needs is political consensus and a collective will to implement the endorsed and adopted counter-terrorism measures. The threat of terrorism that has bedevilled South Asia can be best ameliorated through cooperation at various levels. Mainly, India and Pakistan must come together because neither can tackle this problem unilaterally. But more importantly, as long as one country's terrorist is another country's freedom fighter, the prospects of an effective regional counter-terrorism strategy will remain dim.

## References

"2009 Report on Terrorism" at http://www.nctc.gov/witsbanner/docs/2009_report_on_terrorism.pdf.

"9/11 Commission Report" at http://govinfo.library.unt.edu/911/report/911Report.pdf.

Arpana Pandey, "South Asia Counter-terrorism Policies & Postures after 9/11", at http://www.satp.org/satporgtp/publication/faultlines/volume15/Article4.htm.

B. Raman, *"Countering terrorism in India," South Asia Analysis Group*, Paper no. 3384, September 03, 2009 at http://www.southasiaanalysis.org/%5Cpapers34%5Cpaper3384.html.

"Country Reports on Terrorism" at http://www.state.gov/s/ct/rls/crt/.

Daniel L. Byman, "*The Changing nature of State sponsorship of Terrorism,*" *Saban Center Analysis Paper*, Number 16, May 2008.

Eric Rosand, Naureen Chowdhury Fink, Jason Ipe, "Countering Terrorism in South Asia: Strengthening Multilateral Engagement," *A Report of the Center for Global Counterterrorism Cooperation and International Peace Institute*, May 2009.

"Human Development Report 2009" at http://hdr.undp.org/en/media/HDR_2009_EN_Complete.pdf.

Lisa Curtis, "Denying Terrorists Safe Haven in Pakistan," *Heritage Foundation Backgrounder,* No. 1981, October 26, 2006 at http://www.heritage.org/Research/AsiaandthePacific/upload/bg_1981.pdf.

Marvin Weinbaum, "Afghanistan and Its Neighbors," *U.S. Institute of Peace Special Report* 162, June 2006 at http://www.usip.org/pubs/specialreports/sr162.pdf.

SAARC website, http://www.saarc-sec.org.

South Asian Terrorism Portal website, http://www.satp.org/.

# Index